More Praise for
*The Epistle to the Hebrews
and the Seven Core Beliefs of Catholics*

"Shane Kapler's research has made the sometimes dense theology of the Epistle to the Hebrews accessible to virtually every reader. His new book is a concise look at how the promises of God to His people of the Old Covenant are brought to fulfillment in Jesus Christ. I recommend it for parish Bible studies in every diocese in the land."—BISHOP MICHAEL SHERIDAN, Diocese of Colorado Springs

"An enigma to many Christians, the Epistle to the Hebrews comes alive in a new way in the hands of Mr. Kapler. This is not a book to read once and place on the shelf. Wonderfully written, it is a teaching tool that beautifully illuminates how the Epistle loudly proclaims a Catholic message. I learned a great deal from this gem of a book, and so will you. Don't just buy it. Read it!"—MATTHEW LEONARD, Executive Director of the St. Paul Center for Biblical Theology

"Shane Kapler's new book is more than just a look at the Epistle to the Hebrews—it is deeper than just a study, and more meaningful than mere exegesis. In short, Shane has crafted an encounter with the Living Word of God. Get out your highlighter and brace yourself: you are embarking on a journey, accompanied by saints and angels, and thousands of years of Church wisdom. Truly, this is a treasure you will want to revisit with small groups and on your own."—SARAH REINHARD, author of *Word by Word: Slowing Down with the Hail Mary* and SnoringScholar.com

"When I heard that Shane Kapler was writing a book on the Epistle to the Hebrews, I knew I would read it. When I discovered that he was going to use the Epistle to explain the Trinity, Incarnation, Communion of Saints, Eucharist, and other Catholic beliefs, I wanted to read it... NOW! He does an outstanding job of presenting the Epistle to the Hebrews as a primer of Catholic belief. Shane Kapler is a gifted writer, this is a great book, and you need to read it!"—GARY ZIMAK, Catholic speaker and author of *Faith, Hope and Clarity: How to Know God's Will*

"In Shane Kapler's *The Epistle to the Hebrews and the Seven Core Beliefs of Catholics* we encounter a systematic presentation of Catholic theology. This book is for converts ready to go deeper and discover the Catholic faith leaping from the pages of Scripture. It is for all Catholics interested in beginning an in-depth study of the Book of Hebrews. Kapler makes the case for the papacy, the priesthood, the Blessed Trinity, purgatory, the Eucharist, and Church authority through his comprehensive exegesis. There is no superficial analysis here. No use of text to support a pretext. Kapler presents the Catholic faith with grace, strength, beauty, and undeniable fidelity to sacred scripture. Catholics will delight in this book, which once again proves that the Bible is the book of the Church."—DENISE BOSSERT, author of *Gifts of the Visitation*

"Who knew you could learn so much about our Catholic faith in just the thirteen chapters of the Epistle to the Hebrews? In this well-researched and easy-to-understand book (which would make a perfect companion for your personal or group Bible study), Shane Kapler offers an abundance of insights, connecting this epistle with other books of the New and Old Testament, as well as the writings of the Church Fathers, the Catechism, and other magisterial documents. Reading *The Epistle to the Hebrews and the Seven Core Beliefs of Catholics* will deepen your understanding of the Faith of the first Christians—which has been preserved to today, and will persevere through eternity."—ANNA MITCHELL, Producer and News Director of EWTN Radio's *The Son Rise Morning Show*

The Epistle to the Hebrews

&

The Seven Core
Beliefs of Catholics

✛

Shane Kapler

The Epistle
to the Hebrews

&

The Seven Core
Beliefs of Catholics

Foreword by
Kenneth J. Howell

Preface by
Jared Zimmerer

 Angelico Press

✝

For my dear friend and brother,
Andrew Kapler,
to whom I owe so very much.

Matthew 10:40–42

Acknowledgments

God inspired generosity in the hearts of many friends to make this book a reality: Mr. Tony Grossman provided the initial "whisper in my ear"; and my close friend and writing partner, Dr. Kevin Vost, was right on his heels with a copy of St. Thomas Aquinas's *Commentary on the Epistle to the Hebrews* and the exciting idea that we craft complementary books. Deacon Jim Russell opened his voluminous library to me; and longtime friends Michael Vento and Amy Huesgen read and critiqued the manuscript (in Amy's case, as she journeyed through the RCIA process). Thank you to Dr. John Bergsma for his review of chapter three and his insightful suggestions. I am deeply honored and grateful for Dr. Kenneth Howell and Jared Zimmerer's involvement with this project. Finally, I must express my profound gratitude to Ms. Mackenzie Peter, my (unpaid) research assistant, for her incredibly generous gift of time and effort in tracking down resources; this is a far richer work because of her.

CONTENTS

Foreword

In this small book lies an education. In thirty years of teaching in higher education, I experienced something that surprised me over and over again. Students, otherwise intelligent and well-prepared, found reading and understanding ancient documents difficult. At first, I thought this was because of some deficiency in the students, but I soon came to realize that there was more to it. Reading is not as simple as many people suppose. And reading ancient documents, be they from the Bible or any other ancient source, is especially difficult for modern people. Why is this so? I think it is because people today don't have the necessary background to understand most of these documents. The Epistle to the Hebrews is one such document.

The Epistle to the Hebrews is just under five-thousand words long in Greek and yet is one of the most beautiful pieces of literature in the New Testament. Written sometime in the first century, Hebrews remains an enigma to those who do not share its background in Jewish culture. Though we do not know for sure who its author was, it shows remarkable consistency with the other writings of the New Testament. Still, it remains a closed book to many modern Christians as well as others outside Christianity who may wish to understand it. That's where Shane Kapler's work is essential.

There are references and allusions to practices carried on by the early Jewish Christians which would be obscure unless a trusted

---

* Angelico Press wishes to thank Dr. Howell for contributing Forewords to both *The Epistle to the Hebrews and the Seven Core Beliefs of Catholics* and Dr. Kevin Vost's complementary volume, *The Porch and the Cross*. Taken together, these works seek to show how Providence made use of divine revelation to ready the Jew, and philosophy the Gentile, to receive and live the fullness of the truth revealed in Christ. The modern Christian requires both solid philosophical reasoning and unmitigated faith in God's word to undertake the New Evangelization and return the western world to its Foundation; may these two works be means toward that end.

guide led the reader through every nook and cranny to understand the full meaning of the text. Kapler takes great pains to explain the many references and much of the language of this Letter so as to make it comprehensible to the modern reader. In the process the reader learns the art of reading more carefully and meaningfully so that he is able to apply that acquired skill to other writings from antiquity. One example has to do with the quotations from the Old Testament. Students of Hebrews have long known that the author uses the Septuagint as the source of his quotations. The Septuagint was the primary Greek translation of the Hebrew Old Testament text that was in use among Jews in the first century. This is important to understand because sometimes the Septuagint translation differs from the Massoretic text on which most modern English translations of the Hebrew are based. Kapler's explanations help the reader understand why there are differences between the two.

More importantly, Shane Kapler explains references to practices of these early Christians whose meaning would certainly escape moderns were it not for someone to elucidate them. One such practice alluded to in the text of Hebrews is the Eucharistic celebration, or what today we call the Mass. Many readers have never seen these meanings in the text of Hebrews. I know I did not. As a former Protestant who read the Epistle to the Hebrews many times, I never saw references to "the blood of Christ" (see Heb. 9:12–14; 10:19–20), to the altar (Heb. 13:10) and to the heavenly choir (12:22–24) as having anything to do with Christian worship. Yet, once I understood that the early Christians celebrated the Lord's Supper every week (cf. 1 Cor. 11:17–34), and that they saw the Eucharistic elements as the true body and blood of Christ (see Ignatius of Antioch, Letter to the Smyrneans, ch. 7), then I understood how the references in Hebrews above have a deeper meaning than I thought.

There is something rewarding about understanding more deeply something that one thought he already understood. It can be unsettling, but it can also open new windows on truth. Reading Shane Kapler's explanations of the Epistle to the Hebrews may be that kind of experience for many. There is nothing more needed today than trusted guides who can elucidate the meaning of biblical literature. Even Alighieri Dante needed a guide (Virgil) to help him understand the meaning of Purgatory, Hell, and Paradise. In all things divine, each of us needs trusted guides. Kapler seeks to elucidate seven core beliefs of Catholicism evident in this biblical epistle. He is a trustworthy guide.

At the center of the Epistle to the Hebrews stands the same person who is the center of the Catholic Faith, Jesus Christ. Without him, the Catholic Faith falls apart. He is the hub of the wheel which revolves around him as the center. The forces of Catholicism are centripetal, always tending toward the Center who is Christ. Why is this so? Because the Catholic Faith derived this truth from the Epistle to the Hebrews.

KENNETH J. HOWELL

Preface

Cultures and civilizations across the ages and globe can often find agreement on one of the most important factors of being a living, human being, something that is so dear to our very core that the delineating dissimilarities fall flat at the feet of this one congruent aspect of daily living: relationship. The Hebrews held their relationship to the one, true God as the epitome of human purpose and fulfillment. The ancient Greeks and Romans held relationship as the foundational principle of sound reasoning and dialogue in order to perfect their ideals of virtue. And indeed, I must gleam the profound importance of a friendship such as mine with the likes of Kevin Vost and Shane Kapler. Through the common bond of constant search for truth and finding it in the heart of Christ incarnate, I have been able to form a companionship with these two men that has led to sound communal reasoning and recognition of the Divine reality within God's revealed word. Their dynamic duo of literary works—Shane's *The Epistle to the Hebrews and the Seven Core Beliefs of Catholics*, and Dr. Vost's *The Porch and the Cross*—focus on the prominence of faith and reason, which St. John Paul II called the "two wings of a dove." It brings to mind the image of an ancient Stoic sitting at the foot of Mount Olympus, having a reasoned and revelatory discussion with one of the ancient Hebrew prophets, as he looks to the skies above Mount Zion!

Kevin Vost has become a leading voice in promulgating the wisdom of the great Doctor of the Church, St. Thomas Aquinas. Thomas had a deep love of the Greek and Roman philosophers. It is in the spirit of Thomas's great mind that Kevin dives into the lives and lessons of a few of the prodigious Stoics. With the Church, Kevin resoundingly affirms that truth is truth, no matter who says it. And

* This preface also appears in Kevin Vost's *The Porch and the Cross*.

indeed, the Stoics Kevin discusses knew a great deal of rational, God-given truth; so it is of utmost importance that we continue their legacy of consistently searching for that which will fill our lives with purpose. Kevin, in his uniquely personable writing style, does an incredible job bringing to life the instructions of men who lived nearly 2,000 years ago! It is as if they were writing for our time and our culture, a vivid demonstration of truth's timeless nature.

Personally, I have read quite a bit of the Stoics, but I must admit that I have never had their lessons presented in such a relatable and subjective way. With Kevin revealing a bit about these men's lives, and then relating their message to the indomitable Catholic faith, I found myself coming to revere these men on a much deeper level. I gained even more respect for what they were able to accomplish with natural human reason. I think the most important message, the one that simply oozes from *The Porch and the Cross*, is that the ideals of proper living, loving, and thinking in which these Stoics were so well-versed ought to be a guiding light in a time such as ours. The time in which these teachers lived is more similar to our time than what one might think: morals were washed over with relativism; expressions of love were seen as commerce; and the desire for comfort trumped the necessity of virtue. And yet these men stood tall and strong against such a wave of weakness, preaching the truth that they were able to identify as a gift from God. From Kevin's relating of each of these Stoic lessons to the message of the Cross of Christ—and the Church established by Christ's sacrifice— we see that ultimate wisdom and knowledge of human nature and proper living are ultimately fulfilled in searching for and modeling our own lives off of the discipleship of Jesus, which guarantees our own crosses. It seems that the Stoics would be right next to the likes of St. Thomas Aquinas, cheering us on to pick up our crosses and embrace the struggle of right living in accordance with reason to become the virtuous images of God we were created to be. Which then brings me to the next book in our forceful duet, Shane Kapler's *Hebrews and the Seven Core Beliefs of Catholics*.

While I may be commenting on Shane's book second in this preface, it is in accordance with the practice of presenting ideas in their order of importance. As St. John Paul II so fittingly explained, "The lesson of history in this millennium now drawing to a close shows that this is the path to follow: it is necessary not to abandon the passion for ultimate truth, the eagerness to search for it or the audacity to forge new paths in the search. It is faith which stirs reason to move beyond all isolation and willingly to run risks so that it may attain whatever is beautiful, good and true. *Faith thus becomes the convinced and convincing advocate of reason.*"[1] It is faith that ultimately fulfills what philosophy cannot. It is similar to running a race: when nearing the end, there is nothing left in your physical tank, and it takes something beyond natural inclination to push ahead and finish strong. This is where the faith presented in the Letter to the Hebrews can instruct the accomplished and even mountainous wisdom of the Stoics. Faith is more than just the icing on the cake, it is the yeast which makes it rise!

Shane's unbelievable depth of knowledge regarding Catholicism's first-century Jewish roots was first unveiled in his book *Through, With, and In Him: The Prayer Life of Jesus and How to Make It Our Own*. This new work, expounding upon the seven core beliefs of Catholics as the fulfillment of God's revelation to the Jewish people, concretizes my respect for Shane's work, and my adoration for God's plan overflows! As Catholic Christians we desire to fulfill our Lord's command of "One Faith, One Lord, One Baptism" (Eph. 4:5). A thorough knowledge of our Hebrew ancestors allows us to find common ground with our Protestant brothers and sisters in Sacred Scripture. By unveiling Catholicism's core beliefs within the pages of Scripture—most particularly the reality of Christ's True Presence in the Holy Eucharist and the authority of our ordained leaders—Shane gives us the tools to have a deeper, more significant discussion about the true Church of Jesus Christ. This book offers more than just a profounder understanding of our Jewish roots; it proposes a mental removal of the veil of the Holy of Holies—completing the Jewish understanding of salvation with the exposed and tangible new sanctuary of Christ's body and bringing Jewish faith and the practice thereof to its definitive fulfillment.

1. *Fides et Ratio* (emphasis added).

By continuously linking the rituals and beliefs of the Hebrew people to the written word of God in the Book of Hebrews, Shane boldly indicates the undeniable bond between the Chosen People and the New Covenant in Christ Jesus. The Letter to the Hebrews is a powerful work, surrounded by mystery and containing such striking verses as 4:12: "Indeed, the word of God is living and effective, sharper than any two-edged sword, penetrating even between soul and spirit, joints and marrow, and able to discern reflections and thoughts of the heart." In a truly Catholic spirit, this book builds upon the great prophets of old; in reading it you will find yourself immersed in a world that integrates the best of the ancient with the core of faith in Christ.

I am proud to say that I have been a co-author with these two gentlemen of reason and faith, but I am even more honored to say that I call them friends. When we came together to write *Man Up! Becoming the New Catholic Renaissance Man*, I knew that these two men were gifted and magnetic in their writing and their characters. I can't recommend these two new books enough. I challenge you to do your best to see how God works in the history of mankind through and with the great minds of the past, as well as through his own revelation to his chosen ones. As Christians, as human beings, we must do our part in searching out the heights and the depths of truth. We can do so with the gift of natural human reason so long as it is wrapped in and elevated by the grace of faith. In this way, we can discover the horizon that St. John Paul II desired all of us to reach: "Only within this horizon of truth will people understand their freedom in its fullness and their call to know and love God as the supreme realization of their true self."[2]

JARED ZIMMERER

---

2. *Fides et Ratio*, 107.

Introduction

In many and various ways God spoke of old to our fathers by the prophets, but in these last days he has spoken to us by a Son....
~ Hebrews 1:1–2

✝

The Epistle to the Hebrews has always commanded my attention. Given the role that Judaism played at the beginning of my own conversion, it was probably inevitable. Hebrews, more so than any other book of the New Testament, focuses upon the way Christ brought the Old Covenant to fulfillment. What I could not have foreseen in the early days of my conversion was how my appreciation of the book would increase with the passage of years. I certainly could not have predicted that I would come to view its thirteen short chapters as a syllabus for communicating the essentials of the Catholic Faith.

I realize that the majority of Christians reading Hebrews would not characterize it as a primer in Catholic belief. It wasn't apparent to me on my first, or even fifth, reading of the text. It was only after I began to immerse myself in the Catholic Church's rich theological patrimony and its Jewish roots that I came to view Hebrews as an ideal, biblical means for introducing and expounding upon Catholicism's core convictions. Ultimately, Hebrews reveals the Trinitarian "shape" of our Faith—that God the Son became man to lift us up into his *own relationship* with the Father, in the Spirit. Hebrews show us how the Lord Jesus employs Scripture, Tradition, the communion of saints, the authority of the Church's shepherds, the Eucharist, and other sacraments to bring us to this glorious end. Sharing this vision with you in the pages that follow is incredibly exciting; but before we launch into our study of the text, we need to establish a *context* for understanding Hebrews' overall message.

A People Persecuted

Today, Christians in the Western world are starting to experience discomfort. Our moral convictions are under attack by the culture at large, and those who remain faithful to the tenets of our religion are increasingly characterized as backward, overly judgmental, and mean-spirited. We in the West are not being martyred, but we are facing increased societal pressure—in the form of civil lawsuits and governmental attempts at coercion—to compromise our beliefs. The conflict has made its way into families, creating arguments and division.

The first Christians—the Jewish men and women who recognized Jesus as Israel's Messiah—were subjected to these pressures and worse at the hands of a significant number of leaders in Jewish society. The Epistle to the Hebrews was written to strengthen those first believers against the temptation to abandon their faith in Christ. I want to make it absolutely clear, here at the beginning of this discussion, that no one should take this review of events in the first century as encouraging ill-will between Christians and Jews today. Nothing could be further from my intention, or the intention of Hebrews' first-century author. At the time of the epistle's writing, Judaism and Christianity were not separate religions; Christianity was a movement within Judaism known as "The Way" (Acts 9:2; 19:23). Hebrews was written to encourage *one group of Jews*, experiencing persecution from *another group of Jews*, to remain faithful. The book does have a message for today's reader, but it certainly isn't one of anti-Semitism.

What was the *inter*-Jewish strife that occasioned Hebrews' writing? Jesus had been denounced by the high priest and ruling council, the Sanhedrin, and handed over for execution by the Romans. When his apostles suddenly began proclaiming his resurrection and baptizing and teaching in his name, the Jewish leadership was incensed. When a man or woman professed Jesus as Messiah and started joining the apostles for the "breaking of the bread," or Eucharist (Acts 2:46), it drew opposition. As Jesus had predicted: "a man's foes will be those of his own household" (Matt. 10:36); "They will put you out of the synagogues; indeed, the hour is coming when whoever kills you will think he is offering service to God"

(John 16:2). The Acts of the Apostles, the New Testament's brief history of the early Church, gives several examples:

• Peter and John were arrested and censured by the Sanhedrin (4:1–22).

• The Sanhedrin imprisoned the Twelve Apostles overnight, had them beaten, threatened, and then released (5:17–40).

• The deacon Stephen was hauled before the Sanhedrin and then stoned to death (7:8–60).

• A "great persecution" of the Church in Jerusalem. All but the apostles fled to Judea and Samaria. "Saul laid waste the Church, and entering house after house, he dragged off men and women and committed them to prison" (8:3).

• The high priest sent Saul to the synagogues of Damascus, with letters authorizing him to arrest believers in Christ and transport them to Jerusalem (9:1–2).

• When the newly converted Paul preached in the synagogues of Damascus, a plot was hatched to kill him, in which even the governor of the city participated (9:23–25).

• Herod Agrippa I, the ruler of Palestine from AD 41–44, beheaded the Apostle James and had Peter imprisoned (12:1–5).

• Paul and Barnabas were driven out of Antioch of Pisidia after synagogue leaders incited Gentile authorities against them (13:42–52).

• In Iconium, conversions sparked a Jewish-Gentile plot to stone Paul and his fellow evangelist, Barnabas (14:4–6).

• Hostile Jews from Antioch and Iconium arrived in Lystra, stoned Paul, and left him for dead (14:19).

• Paul made a convert of the synagogue-ruler in Thessalonica. Hostile Jews raided the ruler's home, and hauled him and others before the city magistrate with the charge, "They are all acting against the decrees of Caesar, saying there is another king, Jesus" (17:1–9).

• Jews from Thessalonica arrived in Beroea, incited a crowd, and forced Paul to leave the city (17:10–15).

• The Roman Emperor Claudius expelled all Jews from Rome (18:2). The Roman historian Suetonius recorded that this was because the Jews "were constantly engaging in riots at the instigation of Chrestus"—probably meaning in reaction to early Jewish-Christian missionaries' proclamation of Christ in Rome's synagogues.[3]

• Jews near Corinth brought Paul before the proconsul Gallio, for "persuading men to worship God contrary to the law." When the case was dismissed, a mob beat the synagogue-ruler (who had come to faith in Christ) in retaliation (18:12–17).

The Epistle to the Hebrews was written to Jewish Christians living in such an atmosphere. Both external and internal evidence point to its composition in the middle of the first century. Externally, we find Clement of Rome already drawing from Hebrews in chapter 36 of his *Letter to the Corinthians* (ca. AD 96). Internally, the author of Hebrews speaks of the animal sacrifices under the Mosaic Covenant as a present reality (Heb. 7:11–13:13). The author claimed that the Old Covenant with its sacrificial system "*is becoming* obsolete and growing old [and] is ready to vanish away" (Heb. 8:13). Those sacrifices ended in AD 70, when Rome destroyed Jerusalem's Temple (an event prophesied by Jesus). It is logical to date the epistle prior to that event.[4]

Authorship and Canonicity

The epistle tells us neither the name of its author nor its original recipients, although we can draw inferences. The author is clearly a figure of some authority within the early Christian community, as he expects his words to receive a hearing. It closes with the mention of Timothy, presumably the traveling companion of the Apostle Paul (Heb. 13:23).[5] In the oldest surviving collection of Paul's writ-

---

3. Suetonius, *Claudius* 25.4, quoted in Peter J. O'Brien, *The Letter to the Hebrews* (Grand Rapids, MI: Wm. B. Eerdmans Publishing Co., 2010), 17.

4. Luke Timothy Johnson, *Hebrews: A Commentary (The New Testament Library)* (Louisville, KY: Westminster John Knox Press, 2006), 38–39.

5. Hebrews 13:24 adds, "Those from [*apo*] Italy send you greeting"; but we have no way of knowing how these Italians were known to the recipients. The Greek

ings, dated to AD 200, Hebrews was placed immediately after the Epistle to the Romans.[6] The eastern half of the Church attributed it to Paul throughout the early centuries, with the exception of Origen, the great third-century exegete. He found the thought, but not the style, consistent with Paul's other epistles, and postulated that it had been written by someone in Paul's immediate circle, such as Luke. (Over time, others among Paul's collaborators have been suggested: Barnabas, Silas, Priscilla or Aquila.) In the western half of the Church, doubts over Hebrews' authorship led to doubts about its inclusion among the New Testament books, and it is not found in the earliest attempt at an authoritative list, the *Muratorian Fragment*.[7] The epistle was, however, recognized as canonical by influential western churchmen such as Jerome and Augustine. By the end of the fourth century it was held to be inspired by east and west, and nearly all attributed it to the Apostle Paul.

At the time of the Reformation questions were again raised regarding Hebrews' authorship and its inclusion in the New Testament. Martin Luther, in the preface for his German translation, referred to it as "a marvelously fine epistle," while still insisting that "we cannot put it on the same level with the apostolic epistles."[8] Luther suggested that Apollos, mentioned in Acts 19 and 1 Cor. 3, was the author. For almost a century Lutheran scholars debated Hebrews' inclusion among the books of the New Testament.[9] Calvin, and others in the Reformed tradition, accepted Hebrews on an equal footing with other New Testament works; and fortunately, Lutheran scholars came to as well.

---

preposition *apo* can identify someone's original place of origin as well as where they are living at present. We cannot be sure if our author was writing from Italy to an outside Jewish-Christian community, or to Jewish Christians in Italy. See Craig R. Koester, *Hebrews: A New Translation with Introduction: The Anchor Bible* (New York: Doubleday, 2001), 35.

6. Ibid., 3.

7. Appendix I contains a chart showing the development of the New Testament canon over the first four centuries.

8. Craig R. Koester, *Hebrews*, 58.

9. Ibid.

Modern scholarship, both Catholic and Protestant, is close to unanimous in concluding that Hebrews was not written by the Apostle Paul. Most scholars, like Origen in the third century, recognize a connection to Paul in terms of subject matter but hold that the author's literary style and vocabulary are markedly different.[10] With almost two thousand years between us and the author, there is no way to be absolutely sure. Suffice to say that whoever he was, we Christians believe he was inspired by the Holy Spirit, and as such, the words are ultimately those of God Himself.

The original recipients of the epistle, given its focus on the worship under the Mosaic covenant, were undoubtedly from a Jewish background. To think that they were part of the Christian community in Palestine is reasonable; but the Acts of the Apostles recorded persecutions throughout Mediterranean Jewish communities, and the epistle could have been addressed to any of them. The addressees had already experienced public "abuse and affliction," the plundering of their property, and imprisonment (Heb. 10:32–34); and there was every reason to expect more trouble in the future. Some were tempted to renounce Christ and his Church and return to their family and friends in the synagogue and Temple.

The author reminds them that to do so would be a betrayal of Christ and dash their hopes of salvation. Jesus has inaugurated a new covenant with a heavenly, eternal reward. That glory outweighs any suffering Christians endure. They were following in the footsteps of Christ himself, making their way to the Father's throne by way of the Cross.

The Present Work

In the process of encouraging his original audience, the inspired author encourages you and me as well; and he speaks to us about the deepest mysteries of the Faith—what I call the seven core beliefs of Catholics. I refer to them in this way because of their centrality in

---

10. See the concise, meaty discussion in Albert Vanhoye, *Structure and Message of the Epistle to the Hebrews* (Rome: Editrice Pontificia Universita Gregoriana, 1989), 3–4.

the living of the Faith and because all subsequent Catholic beliefs seem to rest upon them:[11]

1. The Trinity

2. Jesus's full humanity

3. The Word of God (written and unwritten)

4. Salvation

5. The communion of saints

6. The Eucharist (symbol of the whole sacramental life)

7. The authority of our ordained leaders

God does not intend these gifts for Catholics alone, but for all Christians. May this study of the Epistle to the Hebrews, God's written word, help facilitate their full acceptance.

If you have never read the Epistle to the Hebrews, I recommend that you do so now, in its entirety, before beginning chapter one. Keep an eye open for the seven core beliefs as you do. Then come back and allow me to walk through the epistle with you, helping you to see it through the eyes of its original Jewish readers. When you do, I believe that you too will see how Catholic belief and worship is nothing less than the full flowering of God's revelation to Israel.

I hope that after finishing this book you will make a study of my friend Dr. Kevin Vost's *The Porch and the Cross: Ancient Stoic Wisdom for Modern Christian Living*. Where my work focuses upon Christian doctrine and the way God prepared Israel for Christ's advent, Dr. Vost's work explores Christian ethics and how Stoic philosophy acted as a preparation for the Gospel among the Greeks and Romans. Together, we hope these works contribute to an increased appreciation of God's activity in history, better knowledge of our forerunners, and an appreciation of the truth—wherever or however partially it may be found.

---

11. "In Catholic doctrine there exists an order or 'hierarchy' of truths, since they vary in their relation to the foundation of the Christian faith" (*Catechism of the Catholic Church*, 90).

1

The Trinity

HEBREWS, CHAPTERS 1–3

In times past, God spoke in partial and various ways to our ancestors through the prophets; in these last days, he spoke to us through a son, whom he made heir of all things and through whom he created the universe, who is the refulgence of his glory, the very imprint of his being, and who sustains all things by his mighty word.

⁓Hebrews 1:2–3[1]

In the Beginning

To combat the temptation to apostasy, our author leads with the strongest argument possible: the divinity of Christ. Jesus did not deliver God's message in the manner of a prophet. He did so as the Son, the perfect image of the Father, and creator of the universe. We find these same thoughts linked, also in quick succession, in the Gospel of John and in Paul's Epistle to the Colossians:

> In the beginning was the *Word*, and the Word was with God, and the Word *was God*. He was in the beginning with God; all things were made through him, and without him was not anything made that was made. (John 1:1–3)

> He is the *image of the invisible God*, the first-born of all creation; for in him all things were created, in heaven and on earth, visible and invisible.... (Col. 1:15–16)

Israel's monotheistic faith, over a millennium old, was the recipient of a new revelation: The God who revealed Himself to Abraham, Isaac, Jacob, and Moses as the *one*, true God is not a singularity, but

---

1. *New American Bible*, revised edition.

a *plurality*. It was something completely unforeseen, although with hindsight we can glimpse foreshadowing in God's prior revelations to Israel.

In the Old Testament,[2] for instance, the most common designation for "God," used over two thousand times, is *Elohim*. It is a plural word (indicated by its ending, *-im*), which interestingly, in all but three instances is followed by a singular verb.[3] It was generally interpreted as a "plural of majesty"—a reference to God's immensity and incomprehensibility.[4]

Genesis' first creation story offers us more food for thought: "Then God said, 'Let *us* make man in our image, after our likeness. . . .' So God created man in his own image, in the image of God he created *him*; male and female he created *them*. And God blessed them, and God said to them, 'Be fruitful and *multiply*'" (Gen. 1:26, 28).[5] It is as if the union of man and woman, and their resultant fruitfulness, is an image of God. Prior to those words in Genesis we read how "the *Spirit* of God was moving over the face of the waters"; and God created by means of His Word: "And God *said*, 'Let there be. . .'" (Gen. 1:2–3).

We might also note the use of the Hebrew word *echad* in the *Shema*, the creed recited by Jews twice daily. Christians are familiar with its first words, which Jesus identified as the greatest commandment: "Hear, O Israel: The LORD our God is one [*echad*] LORD; and you shall love the LORD your God with all your heart, and with all your soul, and with all your might" (Deut. 6:4). *Echad* almost always means numeric oneness, but it can also refer to the oneness of unity,[6] as in Genesis' second creation story: "Therefore man leaves his father and his mother and clings to his wife, and they become one [*echad*] flesh" (Gen. 2:24).

---

2. Hereafter, "Old Testament" will be designated OT.

3. Robert R. Girdlestone, *Synonyms of the Old Testament* (Grand Rapids, MI: Wm. B. Eerdmans Publishing Co., 1948), 19.

4. Ibid., 22.

5. Jewish interpreters explain Gen. 1:26 either as an example of the "plurality of majesty" or as God confiding His plans to the angels.

6. James Strong, *A Concise Dictionary of the Words in the Hebrew Bible* (New York: Abingdon Press, 1890), 10.

In the New Testament, the most fertile stream of OT thought for explaining Christ's divine preexistence seems to have come from the Jewish wisdom literature. There wisdom was personified as a living being, Lady Wisdom, present with God before creation and his agent therein. The author of Hebrews borrows the language of the OT's Wisdom of Solomon to describe the preexistent Son:

"[The Son] is the refulgence of his glory, the very imprint of his being, and who sustains all things by his mighty word." (Heb. 1:3)

"For [Wisdom] is a breath of the power of God, and a pure emanation of the glory of the Almighty... a reflection of eternal light, a spotless mirror of the working of God, and an image of his goodness . . . while remaining in herself, she renews all things. . . ." (Wis. 7:25–27)

The Wisdom of Solomon appears to have been employed for this same purpose in the Gospel of John (Wis. 9:16–17; John 3:12–13). The OT books of Proverbs and Sirach also provided elements useful for Jewish Christians trying to express their faith in Christ. In those works Wisdom spoke of herself as coming forth from God in the manner of a child from a parent, and being his partner in the work of creation:

"The LORD created [*qanah* in Hebrew, also translated "engendered, conceived"; Gen. 4:1] me at the beginning of his work, the first of his acts of old. / Ages ago I was set up, / at the first, before the beginning of the earth./ When there were no depths I was brought forth /. . . . When he established the heavens, I was there / when he drew a circle on the face of the deep / when he made firm the skies above /. . . then I was beside him, like a master workman; / and I was daily his delight / rejoicing before him always. . . ." (Prov. 8:22–30)

"I came forth from the mouth of the Most High, / the *first-born* before all creatures. / *I ordained* that an unfailing light/ should arise in the heavens, / and I covered the earth like a mist. / I dwelt in high places, / and *my throne was in a pillar of cloud.* Alone I have made the circuit of the vault of heaven / and have walked in the depths of the abyss. (Sir. 24:3–5)[7]

Passages such as these provided the first converts with a scriptural means for speaking to their relatives who had not yet come to faith in Jesus. God had culled the Jewish people from a polytheistic world and spent centuries confirming them in their recognition of Him as the one, true God. Until that truth was firmly established, all God deemed appropriate to give were small clues as to the plurality of Persons within the Godhead. That *Elohim* would reveal Himself as three distinct Persons, perfectly united in the oneness of the divine nature, was unexpected to say the least. Once that revelation was made, however, and a person came to believe, the author of Hebrews was at pains to show that it could not be denied without jeopardizing one's salvation.

The Son, Superior to All Created Mediators

Precisely because Jesus is divine, he is the ultimate mediator with the Father. Throughout the Old Testament, angels mediated God's messages to the Jewish people. The Son, however, is infinitely superior to them; and our author marshals a number of OT verses to support his claim:

For to what angel did God ever say,
"You are my Son,
 today I have *begotten* you" [Ps. 2:7]. . . .
And again, when he brings the *first-born* into the world, he says,
"Let all God's angels *worship him*" [Deut. 32:43].
Of the angels he says,
"Who makes his angels winds,
 and his servants flames of fire" [Ps. 104:4].
But of the Son he says,
"*Your throne, O God*, is for ever and ever,
 the righteous scepter is the scepter of your kingdom.

---

7. For further discussion of the use of personified Wisdom in explaining the preexistence of the Son, I refer you to Lawrence Feingold, *The Mystery of Israel and the Church, Vol. II: Things New and Old* (St. Louis: The Miriam Press, 2010), 150–154; and Gerald O'Collins, *Christology: A Biblical, Historical, and Systematic Study of Jesus* (New York: Oxford University Press, 1995), 37–46.

You have loved righteousness and hated lawlessness;
therefore *God*, your God, *has anointed you*
with the oil of gladness beyond your comrades" [Ps. 45:6–7].
And,
"You Lord founded the earth in the beginning,
and the heavens are the work of *your hands*;
they will perish, but you remain;
they will all grow old like a garment. . . .
But you are the same,
and *your years will never end*" [Ps. 102:25–27].

(Heb. 1:5–13)

The honor given to the human race when the Son became man calls for a strong response on our part: "[W]e must pay the closer attention to what we have heard, lest we drift away from it. For if the message declared by angels [to Moses] was valid and every transgression or disobedience received a just retribution, how shall we escape if we neglect such a great salvation?" (Heb. 2:1–3).[8]

Jesus's greatness soars high above that of Moses, the greatest figure in Israelite history. Moses was God's instrument to deliver the nation from Egypt and communicate his Law. He was "faithful in all God's household," but Jesus is *over that house* as a Son (Heb. 3:5–6). In his divinity, Jesus built the "house," the covenant family, in which Moses served (Heb. 3:3–4). "And we *are* his house *if* we hold fast our confidence and pride in our hope" (Heb. 3:6). We must maintain our "confession" of Christ as Lord and God, and his teaching as the ultimate gauge of reality (Heb. 3:1).

Another Advocate

After masterfully establishing the preeminence of Christ, our author issues a call to faithfulness through an appeal to Israel's past:

Therefore, as the Holy Spirit says, "Today, when you hear his voice, / do not harden your hearts as in the rebellion, / on the day

---

8. Although it is not stated in the OT, the author of Hebrews accepts the Jewish tradition that it was angels, and not God Himself, who delivered the law to Moses at Mount Sinai (Heb. 2:2). We will have more to say about the positive value of tradition in chapter three.

of testing in the wilderness, / where your fathers put me to the test / and saw my works for forty years. / Therefore I was provoked with that generation, / and said, 'They always go astray in their hearts; / they have not known my ways.' / As I swore in my wrath, / 'They shall never enter my rest' [Ps. 95:7–11]." Take care, brethren, lest there be in any of you an evil, unbelieving heart, leading you to fall away from the living God. (Heb. 3:7–12)

Israel's wandering in the desert after its release from Egypt was an incredibly difficult time for the chosen people, and suffering Christians found themselves in an analogous situation.

What I want to draw your attention to is something that may have gone unnoticed in your reading of the last passage. The author of Hebrews introduces his quotation of Scripture with the words, "as the Holy Spirit says. . . ." This means that, in the space of three chapters, our author references all three Persons of the Trinity. Note how the Spirit is not spoken of as a force; he is a Person, a subject of action, who spoke to Israel through the writer of Psalm 95.

The author of Hebrews spoke of the Spirit as Christ himself had. In John's Gospel, at the Last Supper, Jesus spoke to the apostles of the Paraclete, or Counselor, that he and the Father would send them. He is "the Spirit of truth," who will "guide you into all the truth; for he will not speak on his own authority, but whatever he hears he will speak. . . . He will glorify me, for he will take what is mine and declare it to you. All that the Father has is mine. . ." (John 16:13–14). The Spirit shares in all that belongs to the Father and Son.

The most foundational truth into which the Spirit led the Church was a clearer understanding of God's Triune nature. Let us pause to meditate upon this mystery.

The Revelation of Divine Relationships[9]

For too many of us, our instruction regarding the Trinity has amounted to little more than a comparison to the three leaves of the

---

9. I have not encountered anyone who writes of the Trinity with the clarity of Frank J. Sheed. I gladly acknowledge my indebtedness to him and encourage you to read his work for yourself: *Theology for Beginners* (Brooklyn, NY: Angelico Press, 2013), 29–50; and *Theology and Sanity* (San Francisco: Ignatius Press, 1993), 47–126.

shamrock. That is tragic, because the *Catechism of the Catholic Church* calls the Trinity "the central mystery of Christian faith and life ... the mystery of God in himself ... the source of all the other mysteries of faith, the light that enlightens them ... the most *fundamental* and *essential* teaching in the 'hierarchy of the truths of faith'" (CCC 234). The revealed truth that there are "three Persons in one God" is not just a formula to be acknowledged and relegated to a mental shelf. It is the most sublime, most beautiful truth ever made known. The Son and Spirit, and their union with the Father, were revealed in the process of accomplishing humanity's salvation. We, the faithful in the pews, need to penetrate this mystery more deeply; and I suggest that we begin where God himself did—in his revelation to Israel.

God showed himself to the patriarchs, Moses, and the prophets as being one, eternal, omnipotent, and omniscient. We saw, at the beginning of our chapter, how John's Gospel identifies Jesus, the Son, as God's Word (John 1:1). For us human beings, to whom John's Gospel was addressed, words express our intellects, our knowledge. The Word is an expression of God's knowledge—but knowledge of what? The Word existed before creation—both material (our universe) and immaterial creation (angels). The Word, therefore, is not God's knowledge of creation. Logically, the alternative is to recognize that the Word must be God's knowledge of *himself.* We find this confirmed both by the Apostle Paul, who called Christ "the image of the invisible God" (Col. 1:15), and Hebrews' identification of the Son as the "refulgence of [God's] glory, the very imprint of his being" (Heb. 1:3).[10]

To say that the Word is God's knowledge of himself is a mighty claim. God is, after all, perfect. As a result, his knowledge of himself, his "self-image" if you will, must be a perfect reflection of him. All of God's power, existence, life, etc., must be present in the Word. There is nothing in the divine Thinker that is not also in his divine Thought of himself. If God is a living Person, then so too must his Word be a Person. And just as we could not speak of a

---

10. *New American Bible*, revised edition.

thought existing independent of its thinker, or characterize someone as a "thinker" if he did not have a thought, so God and his Word are distinct but inseparably joined within the one, divine nature.

I realize that the last paragraph may sound rather abstract, so let me rephrase it in more familiar language, in the New Testament's preferred terminology: *God* is a *Son* eternally coming forth from his *Father*. God is one divine Person, eternally coming forth as the image and likeness of Another. The Father continuously "begets" the Son. This is the truth we proclaim at Mass each Sunday in the Nicene-Constantinopolitan Creed:

> I believe in one God,
> the Father almighty,
> maker of heaven and earth,
> of all things visible and invisible.
> I believe in one Lord Jesus Christ,
> the Only Begotten Son of God,
> born of the Father before all ages.
> God *from God*, Light *from Light*,
> *true God* from true God,
> *begotten*, not made, *consubstantial* with the Father; [11]
> Through him all things were made.[12]

The Person we call Father, is a father, properly speaking, or "naturally," only to the Son.

Now, how is the Spirit related to the Father and to the Son? St. Paul wrote that "God's *love* has been poured into our hearts *through the Holy Spirit* who has been given to us" (Rom. 5:5). Since Paul's time, the Church's great theologians have identified the Spirit as the mutual love of the Father and Son.

If the Son proceeds from the Father by way of knowledge, then the Spirit proceeds from Father and the Son via the will. This will is common to Father and Son, the Thinker and his Thought. The

---

11. *Consubstantial* (*homoousion* in Greek, *consubstantialem* in Latin) means "of the same substance." Prior to the English-language revision of the Mass in 2010, it was translated as "one in Being with." *Consubstantial* is more precise and better reflects the Church's Trinitarian faith.

12. *The Roman Missal*, 3rd ed; italics added.

Father and Son purposefully *will* to *give themselves to each other*—totally, completely. (This is what it means to love.) Father and Son give themselves to each other in a perfect rush of Love, communicating all they are. Their Love is living, willing, omniscient, omnipotent. The Love of the Father and Son is a third divine Person.

Jesus identified this Person as the "Holy Spirit." In English we use the term "Spirit" to translate the Hebrew word *ruah*, and the Greek *pneuma*, which both mean "breath." We saw above, when we looked at Genesis' first creation story, how the Spirit of God moved over the primordial waters (Gen. 1:2); and the Old Testament is replete with instances of God's Spirit "coming upon" someone and empowering him to accomplish a momentous task. Jesus completed those partial revelations with the truth of the Spirit's divine Personhood. Just as breath is constitutive of the life of man and woman, so is the Spirit of the inner life of God. Just as a man's heart pounds and his breath quickens when he embraces his beloved, so the Father and Son "breathe" the Holy Spirit upon one another within the embrace of the Trinity.[13] This is what we profess in the Creed:

> I believe in the Holy Spirit, the Lord, the giver of life,
> who proceeds from the Father and the Son,
> who with the Father and the Son is adored and glorified,
> who has spoken through the prophets.[14]

I want to stress that the relations between the Father, Son, and Spirit are *eternal* relations. They did not have a beginning, nor will they have an end. This is the one God. The Father has always known Himself in the Person of the Son, and the Father and Son have always poured themselves out in love to each other in the Person of the Spirit.

Also keep in mind that these three Persons exist within the one, divine nature. I would suggest that your own human nature provides you with an analogy to better understand the mystery. The Book of Genesis told us that men and women were formed in the "image and likeness of God" (Gen. 1:27): Your existence could be

---

13. The theological term for this "breathing" forth of the Spirit is "spiration." The Son is begotten by the Father, and the Spirit is spirated by the Father and the Son.

14. *The Roman Missal*, 3ʳᵈ ed.

said to image the Father; your thought within you, the Son; and your capacity to demonstrate love, proceeding as it does from both your existence and thought, the Spirit. You are an individual being, with an individual human nature, and yet these three aspects coexist within you, flowing out of and completing one another. Take any one of those away and you cease to be you. You are a pale reflection of the Triune God in whom infinite Existence, Knowledge, and Love are intertwined as three divine Persons flowing from, and to, One Another within the one, divine nature.

Sons and Daughters in the Son

God's creation of humanity is mysterious. Why would a God who is already perfect love given and perfect love received create lesser beings such as angels, women, and men? We cannot enrich God. What is our created love in comparison to the infinite love expressed within the Trinity? It depends upon Him for its very existence!

God did not create to enrich himself, but to enrich *us*. The love within the Trinity erupted outward in the creation of other beings upon whom God could pour himself out. When we go back to the Book of Genesis, we discover that "image and likeness" was a way of referring to one's children.[15] When Genesis says that we were made in God's image and likeness (1:26), it teaches that God created us to be sons and daughters. When our first parents sinned, however, they rejected God's fatherhood, forced the Holy Spirit from their souls, and damaged the human nature they passed onto us. Now, instead of souls docile to the Spirit's movements, even the most innocent child comes into the world with a heart not naturally docile to the love of God.

But, as we shall see in chapter four, the waters of baptism change that. In them Jesus unites us to himself, and fills us with his Holy Spirit, so that we too can pour ourselves out in love to the Father.[16]

---

15. "When Adam had lived a hundred and thirty years, he became the father of a son in his own likeness, after his image, and named him Seth" (Gen. 5:3).

16. Note the Trinitarian doctrine implicit in the words of baptism. Jesus instructed the apostles to "make disciples of all nations, baptizing them in the *name* [singular] of the Father, and of the Son, and of the Holy Spirit" (Matt. 28:19).

As audacious as it sounds, we are made "partakers of the divine nature" (2 Pet. 1:4). Now you understand why the Trinity is the most "fundamental and essential teaching in the hierarchy" of Christian truths.[17] Our participation in God's inner, relational life is the reason for Christ's incarnation, the words of Scripture, the Church, and the Eucharist and other sacraments. If we fail to understand what God has revealed to us about Himself, we can still receive the other truths of the Faith, but we are missing their raison d'être and unifying principle.

For the author of the Epistle to the Hebrews, coming to fully share God's life is a prize that outweighs any pain or pleasure this world can offer. Let us take his warning to heart: "Take care, brethren, lest there be in any of you an evil, unbelieving heart, leading you to fall away from the living God. But exhort one another every day, as long as it is called 'today,' that none of you may be hardened by the deceitfulness of sin. For we share in Christ, if only we hold our first confidence firm to the end" (Heb. 3:12–14).

17. CCC 234.

2

The Incarnation

HEBREWS, CHAPTERS 2–5

Since, therefore, the children share in flesh and blood, he himself like-wise partook of the same nature, that through death he might destroy him who has the power of death, that is, the devil.

~ *Hebrews 2:14*

✝

What does Christianity mean when it claims that God became a man? Was Jesus truly human in every way that we are? How could he suffer if he was also divine? How was his death salvific? These are the kinds of questions that the Epistle to the Hebrews will help us answer. Let us begin by revisiting chapter two of the epistle, but this time with our focus on the verses addressing Christ's humanity.

Jesus, Fully Human

I am hard-pressed to find nine verses of Scripture more theologically dense than the following:

> For it was fitting that he, for whom and by whom all things exist, in bringing many sons to glory, should make the pioneer of their salvation [Jesus] perfect through suffering. For he who sanctifies and those who are sanctified have all one origin. That is why he is not ashamed to call them brethren, saying . . . "Here am I, and the children God has given me" [Is. 8:18]. Since therefore the children share in flesh and blood, he himself likewise partook of the same nature, that through death he might destroy him who has the power of death, that is, the devil, and deliver all those who through fear of death were subject to lifelong bondage. For surely it is not with angels that he is concerned but with the descendants of Abraham. Therefore he had to be made like his brethren in every respect, that he might become a merciful and faithful high

priest in the service of God, to make expiation for the sins of the people. For because he himself has suffered and been tempted, he is able to help those who are tempted. (Heb. 2:10–18)

The author proclaims the truth that *God redeems humanity by becoming one with it.* The Son came among us as a new Adam—a new head, a champion for the human race. To save us, he lived through the most severe trials men and women face, but without sin. He took upon himself the suffering our sins deserve and bore it to the grave. But all of this was dependent upon him *truly* becoming a man. As St. Gregory Nazianzus (d. 374) said so succinctly, "That which was not assumed is not healed; but that which is united to God is saved."

The Son's becoming man is what Christianity refers to as the *Incarnation* (from the Latin for "made flesh"). The Son did not surrender his divinity. Rather, Jesus is true God and true man, simultaneously. His divine and human natures are not mixed together in a divine-human jumble, nor is Jesus's humanity simply absorbed into His divinity. Quite the contrary, they remain unconfused. And yet, to meet Jesus is to meet God himself. That human nature, that union of body and soul, belongs to a divine Person. His words and actions are the *human words and actions of God the Son.*

The author of Hebrews stressed that Christ had to "be made like his brethren in every respect." As a man He was not spared any of the fatigue, exertion, etc., experienced by you and me. Jesus's body was as fragile as ours. He knew what it was to be a helpless child, completely dependent upon his mother to be fed and changed. He learned to walk and talk. Even though, in the heights of his soul he had the most intimate, immediate knowledge of the Father,[1] he still had to learn to express his love for the Father in the words and gestures of human prayer.[2] Luke's Gospel tells us that Jesus

1. "For the Father loves the Son and shows him all that he himself is doing. . . ." (John 5:20); "[N]o one knows the Father except the Son and anyone to whom the Son chooses to reveal him" (Matt. 11:27).

2. "The Son of God who became Son of the Virgin learned to pray in his human heart. He learns to pray from his mother. . . . He learns to pray in the words and rhythms of the prayer of his people, in the synagogue at Nazareth and the Temple at Jerusalem" (CCC 2599).

"*increased* in wisdom and in stature, and in favor with God and man" (2:52).

Throughout his earthly life Jesus loved the Father with a human *heart* and obeyed Him with a human *will*. In his human soul the Son said "yes" to everything that he had decided divinely with the Father and the Spirit.[3] The only way Jesus differs from you and me is that his soul does not bear the scars of original sin: he did not come into the world separated from the Father, with the "pull" we feel toward selfishness and sin.[4] His is the human soul of the Son, the one who receives all he is from the Father and pours himself out in a return of love (the Spirit). The author of Hebrews recognized the first movement of Jesus's soul in the words of Psalm 40: "When Christ came into the world, he said, 'Sacrifices and [sin] offerings you have not desired, but a body have you prepared for me.... I have come to do your will, O God'" (Heb. 10:5–7). The Son's human will was perfectly attuned to the divine will. As such, all his actions were manifestations of his love for the Father, and thus performed in the power of the Spirit.

Subject to Trials

We must keep the above points in mind when Hebrews speaks of Jesus being "tempted." We saw this in Hebrews 2:18, quoted above, and it occurs again in chapter four: "For we have not a high priest who is unable to sympathize with our weaknesses, but one who in every respect has been tempted as we are, yet without sinning. Let us then with confidence draw near to the throne of grace, that we may receive mercy and find grace to help in time of need" (Heb. 4:15–16). Taken at face-value, Hebrews seems to say that Jesus, *a divine Person*, was tempted to sin; and that simply isn't possible— God is goodness itself. The apparent contradiction disappears when we dig beneath the surface and discover that the word translated

---

3. CCC 475

4. This inclination to sin is called *concupiscence* (CCC 404–405). That Jesus did not experience concupiscence does not make him less human than us, but more. Concupiscence is a result of humanity's fall from grace. In Jesus we see human nature as it was intended by God in the beginning.

into English as "tempted" (*peirasmos* in Greek) occurs twenty-one times in the New Testament, and in all but one instance (1 Tim. 6:9) it means "trial," "testing," or "ordeal," as opposed to temptation to sin.[5] Jesus knew the discomfort and pain that can result from choosing God's will (for example, Matt. 4:1–4). In fact, because he never succumbed, and thus was never granted relief, he knows that pain more acutely than anyone else. Like the original recipients of the epistle, Jesus had been publicly denounced, arrested, and abused (Heb. 10:32–34; 13:13); and yet he remained faithful to the path marked out for him by the Father. In truth, Jesus endured far, far more than they had (Heb. 12:2–4).[6]

Jesus's whole life was one of redemption, atonement. When God the Son entered the human family, he joined himself in some way to each of us and took it upon Himself to act in our name. As our representative he underwent a baptism of *repentance* at the hands of John (Matt. 3:11, 15). The Spirit drove him into the desert to relive our first parents' testing by Satan and Israel's forty years in the wilderness of Sinai, and he redeemed their sins and failures through his acts of faithfulness.[7] But as the author of Hebrews reminded his readers, the height of Jesus's testing was reached in the Passion:

> In the days of his flesh, Jesus offered up prayers and supplications, with loud cries and tears, to him who was able to save him from death, and he was heard for his godly fear. Although he was a Son, he learned obedience through what he suffered; and being made perfect he became the source of eternal salvation to all who obey him, being designated by God a high priest according to the order of Melchizedek. (Heb. 5:7–10)

In the Garden of Gethsemane, Jesus collapsed to the ground and cried through tears, "Abba, Father, all things are possible to you; remove this chalice from me; yet not what I will, but what you will" (Mk. 14:35–36). Jesus knew the incredible physical suffering that lay ahead, and his human nature recoiled from it. But the sorrow that

---

5. See James T. O'Connor, *The Father's Son* (Boston: St. Paul Books & Media, 1984), 284, n. 20, where Joachim Jeremias's exegetical work is quoted.

6. Craig R. Koester, *Hebrews*, 283.

7. CCC 538–9.

pushed him to the point of death (Mk. 14:34) was fed by something far deeper than the dread of scourging and crucifixion: Jesus stepped into the place of sinners, taking, as it were, the weight of our sins upon his shoulders. He witnessed every betrayal, slander, rape, and murder from history's dawn until its end and offered the Father all the sorrow and contrition that mankind should feel, but does not.[8] Jesus's simple words asking for relief, *but, much more importantly, for the Father's will to be done*, made reparation for mankind's disobedience. Even more importantly, by his obedience Jesus offered the Father the love of which those sins robbed Him. Because Jesus is a divine Person, his actions had infinite merit and more than atoned for humanity's sins. The Father did save him from death, but as Hebrews tells us, it was only after Jesus had "taste[d] death for everyone" (Heb. 2:9).

Achieving His Goal

The author of Hebrews makes the startling claim that Jesus was "made perfect" by obediently accepting suffering, and I would suggest that there are at least two ways in which this is true. First, although Jesus, as the Word made flesh, had poured himself out to the Father from the first instant of his conception, like all men and women he was on a journey. His humanity had a beginning in time and space, and it had a goal—his Passover from this world to the

---

8. Matthew Levering summarized the insights of St. Thomas Aquinas on Christ's interior sufferings: "Christ's penitential love for sinners on the Cross is not weakened, as our sorrow for sin always is, by forgetfulness (allowing ourselves to think about other consoling things), emotional breakdown, or simple lack of apprehension of the profound ugliness of sin in light of the infinite beauty of God's love. Christ cannot and does not hide in these normal ways from the fullness of sin's horror as we can do. Rather, Christ on the Cross intimately (in his human knowing) knows God, and therefore knows exactly what we sinners are rejecting and devaluing. By so knowing, Christ knows the depths of our loss in a way that no person, lacking such knowledge could ever know it. Aquinas explains that Christ's sadness has an unapproachable intensity because of the focus of his sorrow for our sins (a focus conjoined to his focus on God's goodness, in light of which—and only in light of which—our sins take on their true horror)." *Sacrifice and Community: Jewish Offering and Christian Eucharist* (Malden, MA: Blackwell Publishing, 2005), 78.

Father (Lk. 9:31). In each moment of his life, Jesus showed forth, in a human way, the perfect surrender of love that the Son makes to the Father in the divine nature; but at the Cross he crowned and completed this self-offering with the irrevocable giving of his body and soul in death.[9]

The result of that was the Resurrection! The Father raised Jesus from death to an "indestructible life" (Heb. 7:16). The author of Hebrews hears the Father address the risen Jesus in the words of the Psalm, "You are my Son, today I have begotten you" (Heb. 5:5; Ps. 2:7). Hebrews echoes St. Paul, who says that Christ was "*designated Son of God in power according to the Spirit of holiness by his resurrection from the dead*" (Rom. 1:4). The Resurrection was when the Father caused Jesus's Sonship to be *known* by all of creation. I would be remiss if I failed to point out how Hebrews' Christology, its teaching about the Lord Jesus, harmonizes perfectly with what St. Paul wrote to the church in Philippi:

> [A]lthough [Christ Jesus] was in the form of God, he did not count equality with God a thing to be grasped, but emptied himself, taking the form of a servant, being born in the likeness of men. And being found in human form he humbled himself and became obedient unto death, even death on a cross. Therefore God has highly exalted him and bestowed on him the name which is above every other name, that at the name of Jesus every knee should bow, in heaven and on earth and under the earth, and every tongue confess that Jesus Christ is Lord to the glory of God the Father. (Phil. 2:6–11)

I believe that all of this is encapsulated in Hebrews' claim that Jesus's humanity was "made perfect" through his Passion; but there is yet another related level of meaning we need to recognize.

When the writer of Hebrews quotes from the OT, he is using the Greek translation, the Septuagint, completed one hundred years before Christ's birth. (More on this in chapter three.) I mention it now because the Greek word translated here as "perfect," *teleiō*, was used in the Septuagint in reference to priestly ordination. When an

9. Roch A. Kereszty, *Jesus Christ: Fundamentals of Christology* (New York: Alba House, 1991), 319.

Israelite was ordained to the priesthood, his hands were anointed with oil; and when the OT was translated from Hebrew into Greek, *teleiō* was used in place of the Hebrew idiom "fill up the hands." (See Exod. 29:29, 35; Lev. 4:55, 8:33, 16:32, 21:10; Num. 3:3).[10] Bearing that in mind, Hebrews' words take on new significance: "[Jesus] learned obedience through what he suffered; and being *made perfect* he became the source of eternal salvation to all who obey him, *being designated by God a high priest* according to the order of Melchizedek" (Heb. 5:8–9).[11] Now, an explanation of what our author means when he says that Jesus is a priest in the "order of Melchizedek" will have to wait for chapter four. For right now it is enough to understand that not only did God the Son became a man and live a life of perfect love and obedience to the Father in atonement for our sins; but that through his Cross, Resurrection, and Ascension, Jesus made a *priestly* offering to the Father. In Jesus's incarnation, he brought God to humanity; and now, *in the exercise of his high priesthood*, he brings humanity to God.

"Since then we have a great high priest who has passed through the heavens, Jesus, the Son of God, let us *hold fast to our confession*" (Heb. 4:14). Continuing to profess faith in Christ, even when faced with hostility, was essential for Hebrews' original audience, and it remains so for us today. "[E]veryone who acknowledges me before men, I also will acknowledge before my Father who is in heaven; but whoever denies me before men, I also will deny before my Father who is in heaven . . . and he who does not take up his cross and follow me is not worthy of me" (Matt. 10:32–33, 38).

---

10. Kevin B. McGruden, "The Concept of Perfection in the Epistle to the Hebrews," in Eric F. Mason and Kevin B. McCruden, eds., *The Epistle to the Hebrews: A Resource for Students* (Atlanta: Society of Biblical Literature, 2011), 218; Scott Hahn and Curtis Mitch, *The Ignatius Catholic Study Bible: New Testament* (San Francisco: Ignatius Press, 2010), 422.

11. Providentially, in John's Gospel, *tetelestai* (from the same root as *teleio*) was Jesus's final word from the Cross. We see it translated into English as the phrase, "*It is finished*" (John 19:30).

3

The Word of God

HEBREWS, CHAPTERS 4–6

For good news came to us just as to [those who left Egypt under the leadership of Moses]; but the message which they heard did not bene-fit them, because it did not meet with faith in the hearers.... [As God said] through David so long afterward, in the words already quoted, "Today when you hear his voice, do not harden your hearts" [Ps. 95:7]. ⁓*Hebrews 4:2, 7*

✝

When God speaks, it calls for an obedient response from us. In this chapter we will explore God's Revelation to humanity. Our reflection upon the Trinity and the Son's incarnation were necessary prerequisites. As St. John of the Cross notes in his paraphrase of Hebrews 1:2–3, God "has no more to say [to us], because what he spoke before to the prophets in parts, he has now spoken all at once by giving us the All, who is his Son."[1] The Epistle to the Hebrews will introduce us to the two means whereby Christ's teaching is communicated to the world—the written word of God and the authoritative Tradition entrusted to His Church. In the process we will see how this arrangement is the perfection of God's dealings with Israel under the Mosaic covenant.

The Word in Scripture

Christianity is not a "religion of the book" as is Islam, but of the *Word*.[2] John the Apostle wrote of Jesus as the Word of Life, "which we have looked upon and touched with our hands" (1 John 1:1).

1. *The Collected Works of St. John of the Cross*, trans. Kieran Kavanaugh and Otilio Rodriguez (Washington, DC: Institute of Carmelite Studies, 1991), 230.
2. CCC 108.

Scripture, precisely because it is a written record of Christ's revelation—first as the divine Word to the leaders and prophets of Israel, and then as the Incarnate Word to the apostles and people of first century Palestine—is revered by God's people. For the Jewish people, the written word was contained in the scrolls used by those who led them in the liturgies of the temple and synagogue.

The vast majority of Jewish people learned scripture not by reading it, but by hearing it prayed and expounded in the liturgy. Before the advent of the printing press, all written materials had to be copied by hand—a painstaking process for scribes and cost-prohibitive for the average consumer. The greatest obstacle to reading scripture for oneself, however, was the ancient world's abysmally low literacy rate. It is estimated that ninety percent of the population of first-century Palestine could do no more than write their names.[3] This is why in the gospel accounts, when Jesus debated scripture with the temple authorities and scribes, he could ask, "Have you never read?" (e.g., Matt. 12:3, 19:4, 21:16); but when addressing the crowds he would say, "You have heard" (e.g., Matt. 5:21, 27, 33).[4]

The writer of Hebrews refers to his epistle as a "word of exhortation," the term used for a sermon in the synagogue (Acts 13:15).[5] With his extensive quotation of the psalms and prophets, it is a fine example of the way most Jews came to know and understand Scripture. The convictions of the author of Hebrews regarding the written word is seen in the way he introduces quotations: "God says" (Heb. 1:5–6; 5:5; 6:13; 8:5, 8; 10:16); "he has promised" (Heb. 10:36; 12:26); "as the Holy Spirit says" (Heb. 3:7, 10:15); as well as the claim that the OT scriptures allow us to "eavesdrop" on Christ's prayer to

---

3. Timothy Michael Law, *When God Spoke Greek: The Septuagint and the Making of the Christian Bible* (New York: Oxford University Press, 2013), 90. For further discussion of literacy in first-century Palestine, see John P. Meier, *A Marginal Jew: Rethinking the Historical Jesus*, vol. 1 (New York: Doubleday, 1991), 274–8.

4. Law, *When God Spoke Greek*, 90.

5. Gabriella Gelardini, "Hebrews, Homiletics, and Liturgical Scriptural Interpretation," in Eric F. Mason and Kevin B. McCruden eds., *The Epistle to the Hebrews: A Resource for Students* (Atlanta: Society of Biblical Literature, 2011), 121–145; Albert Vanhoye, *Structure and Message of the Epistle to the Hebrews* (Rome: Editrice Pontificia Universita Gregoriana, 1989), 3–6.

the Father (Heb. 2:12–13, 10:5). As the very words of God, the Old Testament scriptures have power. After quoting Psalm 95's warning, "Today, when you hear his voice...," our author continues:

> For the word of God is *living* and *active*, sharper than any two-edged sword, piercing to the division of soul and spirit, of joints and marrow, and discerning the thoughts and intentions of the heart. And before him no creature is hidden, but all are open and laid bare to the eyes of him with whom we have to do. (Heb. 4:12–13)

God's word has the power to cut through the cacophony of voices we hear and the justifications we make to ourselves and confront us with God's truth, the ultimate reality. Scripture has this power because, to use St. Paul's term, it is "inspired" (2 Tim. 3:16).

Inspiration and Inerrancy

It is easy for English speakers to miss the dynamism of Christian belief. Paul spoke of scripture as *theópneustos* (Greek), literally "God-breathed." His word choice evokes Genesis' story of the creation of man: God breathed into the clay he had shaped, transforming it into a "living" being (Gen. 2:7).[6] Hebrews and Paul are one in ascribing a living, active power to scripture. It is truly the word of God, a manifestation of the divine Word.

The mystery of inspiration is analogous to the mystery of the Incarnation. Just as the Father's Word truly became man, like us in all things but sin (Heb. 4:15); so in Scripture the words of God are expressed in the words of men, like human language in all things but error.[7] This truth guards us against the Scylla and Charybdis of modern biblical interpretation—on the one hand, ascribing error to scripture, and on the other, biblical fundamentalism. The former fails to understand scripture's divine character, the latter its human.

---

6. See also John 20:22 and Isaiah 55:11. Ultimately, the mystery of inspiration is related to that of the Incarnation. *Theópneustos* should remind us of the way the Word became flesh in the womb of the Virgin through the power of the Holy *Spirit*, the *Breath* of God.

7. Vatican Council II's *Dogmatic Constitution on Divine Revelation* (*Dei Verbum*), nos. 11, 13.

The Catholic Church has remained adamant that Scripture contains no errors. It is impossible that God, the ground of all reality, would perpetrate error. This extends not just to scripture's religious claims, but to matters of history, etc. As late as 1965, at Vatican Council II, the pope and bishops reaffirmed the Church's ancient faith: "Therefore, since *everything* asserted by the inspired authors or sacred writers *must be held to be asserted by the Holy Spirit*, it follows that the books of Scripture must be acknowledged as teaching solidly, faithfully and without error that truth which God wanted put into sacred writings for the sake of salvation." (*Dogmatic Constitution on Divine Revelation*, 11).[8] Although you will encounter Catholic scripture scholars who claim that Scripture is protected from error only in matters pertaining directly to our salvation, they are not conveying the mind of the Church.[9]

This conviction does not, however, lead to biblical fundamentalism, taking every word of the Bible *literally*, at face-value. On the contrary, because scripture is fully human we have to come to it as we would any piece of literature—actually, as we would a *library* of ancient literature. The Bible is not one book, but seventy-three, written over a period of more than a thousand years. We encounter a wide variety of literary forms: history, prophecy, poetry, hymns, apocalypse, pastoral instruction, etc., each operating according to its own rules. We find literary devices such as idioms, symbolic numbers,[10] anthropomorphisms (as in Exod. 13:3 or Deut. 11:12), and personification (like "Lady Wisdom," discussed in chapter one).

---

8. *Dogmatic Constitution on Divine Revelation*, accessed May 23, 2015, http://www.vatican.va/archive/hist_councils/ii_vatican_council/documents/vat-ii_const_19651118_dei-verbum_en.html.

9. I treated this at some length, especially the claim that this was taught at Vatican Council II, in *The God Who is Love: Explaining Christianity From Its Center* (St. Louis: Out of the Box, 2009), 118–120, and 285–293.

10. Doctor Barbara Organ, for instance, in her *Is the Bible Fact or Fiction?: An Introduction to Biblical Historiography* (New York: Paulist Press, 2004), addressed the use of numbers in biblical chronologies. In 1 Kings 6:1 we are told that the temple was established 480 years after Israel came out of Egypt. When one examines the chronology more minutely it appears that a total of 534 years passed. Organ suggests that patterns were often inherent, and a perfectly acceptable literary device

All of this has to be taken into account before we can properly understand what truth is being asserted in a given passage.

Catholics see no conflict between the truths asserted in Scripture and the truths discovered by science. For example, when we read the creation stories in Genesis we understand that the author did not intend to write a scientific text. (That Genesis contains two creation stories should be a strong indication that neither was intended as a blow-by-blow account of humanity's creation.) The writer's words need not be taken as a scientific statement about the age of the earth, nor a preemptive denial of an evolutionary process at work in the formation of the human body.[11] No: instead, he made use of a genre sometimes called poetic, or symbolic, history.[12] That is not to say that the narrative is false; only that it conveys profound, complex events through much more easily understood symbols. In the first chapters of Genesis, symbols already available in the surrounding culture[13] were used to teach that Yahweh, the God

in ancient chronologies. For Israelites the number forty represented fullness/completion, and so the 480 years leading up to the temple would be symbolic—forty multiplied by Israel's twelve tribes. She continues, "The people of Israel spent forty years in the wilderness (Num.32:13).... David reigned for forty years as did Solomon (1 Kings 2:11; 11:42). Prior to the monarchy, Eli the priest is said to have 'judged' Israel for forty years.... The pattern is especially noticeable in the Book of Judges, where the period of rest from the enemies is measured in forty or eighty years for a total of 200 years.... David and Solomon, as Israel's greatest kings, could not have reigned for less than a full cycle of years" (120).

11. If a Christian thinks that God called forth the human body through evolution that is acceptable, so long as he/she holds that once the body was fully evolved the Lord united a rational soul with it—bringing the first man and woman into existence. As we saw above, it wasn't until the Lord "breathed into his nostrils the breath of life, [that] man became a *living soul*" (Gen. 2:7).

12. Pope St. John Paul II, in his general audience of November 7, 1979, referred to the first three chapters of Genesis as "myth," going on to explain that "the term myth does not designate a fabulous content, but merely an archaic way of expressing a deeper content." William G. Most, *Free From All Error* (Libertyville, Illinois: Prow Books/Franciscan Marytown Press, 1985), 66.

13. The order of creation largely follows the same sequence as that in the *Enuma Elish*, an ancient Babylonian creation myth. Images such as a "plant of life" and a serpent can be found in the Babylonian *Epic of Gilgamesh*. "Genesis, Reading Guide," in *The Catholic Study Bible*, ed. D. Senior, M.A. Getty, C. Stuhlmueller, and J.J. Collins. (New York: Oxford University Press, 1990), 61–62.

of Israel—and He alone—created the earth. Not only that, but He granted man and woman the unheard-of dignity of being made in His image and likeness. That was the message God inspired the human author to write, in words that were intelligible to *his culture*. (Like Christ, the biblical word "took flesh" in a specific time and place.) When fundamentalists fail to perform their due diligence in understanding a text such as Genesis' first chapters, and go on to insist that the Bible teaches that the earth was made in six calendar days, they expose the Faith to unnecessary criticism.

Scripture's inspiration and inerrancy are matters of faith, and Christianity has always held that they pertain to the original, completed texts as they issued forth from God, through the human authors and editors. Inspiration and inerrancy do not protect the text from the errors of later copyists and translators. We must remember that you and I are not reading the *actual* Hebrew, Aramaic, and Greek words that God inspired, but an English translation; and in every translation there is always some degree of *interpretation*. It may surprise you to discover how that was as true for first century Jews and Christians as it is for us today.

The Septuagint

When the author of Hebrews quoted from the Old Testament, he used the Greek translation known as the Septuagint.[14] In the first century, very few Jews outside of the Holy Land spoke Hebrew. Even within Palestine, the Hebrew language had gradually become reserved for religious rites and poetry, with Aramaic (and sometimes Greek) replacing it as the vernacular.[15] (Up until a few decades ago, Catholics had an analogous situation in the way Latin was the language of the Mass, albeit not of daily life.) The language of most people throughout the Mediterranean was Greek, and had

14. "Septuagint" comes from the Greek term for seventy, a reference to the seventy translators said to have worked on the initial translation of the *Torah* (the first five books of Hebrew Scriptures). For this reason you will also see the Septuagint abbreviated as LXX, the Roman numerals for seventy.

15. Albert C. Sunderberg Jr., "The Septuagint: The Bible of Hellenistic Judaism," in Lee Martin McDonald and James A. Sanders, eds., *The Canon Debate* (Peabody, MA: Hendrickson Publishers, Inc., 2002), 89–90.

been since Alexander the Great conquered the known world in the early fourth century BC.

If you have looked up any of the New Testament's quotations of the Old, then you have probably found small discrepancies between the two. This is because our English translations of the OT are made from the Hebrew Masoretic Texts, the oldest complete copy of which dates to the eleventh century AD.[16] When the writers of the New Testament quoted from the OT, eighty percent of the time they did so from the Septuagint, which was used in all of the synagogues outside of Palestine. The Septuagint was even being used within Palestine, in the synagogues of Greek-speaking Jews who immigrated back to the Holy Land. Acts 6:9 refers to one such synagogue in Jerusalem.

The Torah, the first five books of Scripture, was the first to be translated into Greek. This was most likely undertaken in Alexandria, Egypt, around 250 BC. Over the next one hundred fifty years the other books used by Jews in their worship and study were also translated. Both inside and outside of Palestine, new Jewish sacred works were composed in Greek, such as the Wisdom of Solomon and 2 Maccabees, and used alongside the previously written scriptures.

The wording of the Septuagint strikes many as providential, allowing the apostles and other NT writers to expound upon the mysteries of the Faith. Compare the Septuagint text of Psalm 40, used by the author of Hebrews, with that of the Masoretic Text:

16. The Masoretes were groups of Jewish scribes who worked between the seventh and tenth centuries AD. They established a fixed form for the Hebrew Scriptures, clarifying disputed readings. Prior to the work of the Masoretes, written Hebrew had no vowels, which led to confusion in interpretation. Masoretes introduced vowel marks (points) above and below the consonants to clarify the readings. The Masoretes, in effect, determined the meaning of the biblical text for countless generations of Jewish readers. The oldest complete Masoretic text of the Old Testament is called the Leningrad Codex, and is dated to the eleventh century. It is housed in the National Library of Russia in St. Petersburg (formerly Leningrad). Where different interpretations could arise, the Masoretes decided the appropriate reading. Their interpretation dictated how all subsequent generations interpret the Hebrew text. Modern scholars will disagree with the Masoretes at certain points, suggesting other readings: see Timothy Michael Law, *When God Spoke Greek*, 23.

HEBREWS 10:5–7	PSALM 40:6–8, MASORETIC TEXT
[W]hen Christ came into the world, he said, "Sacrifices and offerings you have not desired, / but *a body have you prepared for me*; / in burnt offerings and sin offerings you have taken no pleasure. / Then I said, 'Behold, I have come to do your will, O God,' / as it is written of me in the roll of the book."	Sacrifice and offering you do not desire; / but *you have given me an open ear.* / Burnt offering and sin offering you have not required. / Then I said, "Behold, I come; in the roll of the book it is written of me."

Such examples can be multiplied. Two that immediately come to mind as being of special interest to Christians are Isaiah 7:14 and Psalm 22:17. Compare Matthew's citation from the Septuagint with the Masoretic Text:

MATTHEW 1:22–23	ISAIAH 7:14, MASORETIC TEXT
All this took place to fulfil what the Lord had spoken by the prophet: "Behold a *virgin* shall conceive and bear a son, and his name shall be Emmanuel" (which means, God with us)."	"Look, the *young woman* is with child and shall bear a son, and shall name him Imman-uel." (New Revised Standard Version)

The Hebrew word translated "young woman" is *almah*. Generically it means a "girl of marriageable age," a maiden without a husband, who would quite naturally be considered a virgin (cf. Gen. 24:16).[17] The translators of the Septuagint felt that the Greek word *parthenos* [virgin] best conveyed Isaiah's meaning; and the evangelist Matthew, inspired by the Holy Spirit, assures us that they were correct in doing so.

Psalm 22 is one of the great prophetic psalms. Jesus drew our eyes to it when he prayed its first words from the Cross: "My God, my

17. Stefano Manelli, "The Mystery of the Blessed Virgin Mary in the Old Testament," in Mark Miravalle, ed., *Mariology: A Guide for Priests, Deacons, Seminarians, and Consecrated Persons* (Goleta, CA: Queenship Publishing, 2007), 18–19.

God, why have you forsaken me?" King David penned the psalm a thousand years before Christ's birth. In it, a righteous man suffers: derided by the crowd as if he were abandoned by God (v. 7), his bones out of joint (v. 14), and enemies casting lots for his garments (v. 18). Consider verse seventeen:

SEPTUAGINT	MASORETIC TEXT
[A] company of evildoers encircle me; / they have *pierced* my hands and feet.	A company of evildoers encircles me. / My hands and feet have *shriveled*. (New Revised Standard Version)

You can understand the amazement Greek-speaking Jewish Christians would have felt as they read those words. You might also imagine how those rabbis who vehemently disagreed with the Jewish-Christian belief that Jesus's death and resurrection had been prophesied in Scripture would have felt drawn, perhaps without any forethought, toward a competing textual tradition.

In the first century the texts of the Hebrew Scriptures did not exist in one set form. The discovery of the Dead Sea Scrolls have shown us that there were different versions of the books of Scripture in circulation. The Masoretic text *does* reflect an ancient literary tradition, but it was only *one* of the scriptural traditions in existence prior to AD 200.[18] It wasn't until that time that the Jewish rabbis appear to have definitively set forth which books were to be recognized as scripture and to have begun the process of arriving at a fixed text.[19] The translators of the Septuagint did their work centuries earlier, between 250 and 100 BC. Copies of the first five books of the Bible found among the Dead Sea Scrolls reflect what came to

18. Emanuel Tov, "The Status of the Masoretic Text in Modern Text Editions of the Hebrew Bible: The Relevance of Canon," in *The Canon Debate*, 235–243.

19. Jack N. Lightstone, "The Rabbis' Bible: The Canon of the Hebrew Bible and the Early Rabbinic Guild," in *The Canon Debate*, 178. As Lightstone notes, the earliest rabbinic list of scriptural texts purports to be from the second century, but comes to us via the Babylonian Talmud (*Baba Batra* 14b–15a), written ca. AD 550–600.

be the Masoretic text only forty-eight percent of the time.[20] Some of the scrolls represent the Hebrew texts that lay behind the Septuagint translation. Others reveal even more variants.

In some instances the Septuagint witnesses to a more primitive version of the Hebrew text. The Septuagint's Jeremiah is roughly one-sixth shorter than that found in today's Hebrew Bible, which was apparently expanded by later editors.[21] Samuel is likewise more streamlined in the Septuagint. The story of David and Goliath, for instance, is thirty-nine verses shorter.[22]

Why have I spent some time discussing these issues? Because, even though Scripture is inspired and inerrant, God has made our ability to access it dependent upon a chain of fellow human beings stretching back millennia—from those privileged individuals who first heard His word, to those inspired to begin the process of inerrantly committing it to writing, to those inspired to make additions to the text, to the generations of scribes who copied it, all the way down to the translators who allow it to reach people like us on distant continents, in distant centuries. Scripture does not exist in a vacuum but comes to us through a community of faith; and whether we realize it or not, God has made our ability to hear and read His word dependent upon that community.

The Deuterocanonicals or Apocrypha

If we advance to chapter eleven of Hebrews, we find the author exhorting his readers to faithfulness by recalling the great men and women of the past. Beginning with Abraham, he moves steadily forward through outstanding figures in Jewish history—Isaac, Jacob, Moses, Rahab, David, Samuel—challenging readers to emulate their faith. He continues, "Women received their dead by resur-

20. Timothy Michael Law, *When God Spoke Greek: The Septuagint and the Making of the Christian Bible* (New York: Oxford University Press, 2013), 25. The Septuagint is reflected in the Dead Sea Scrolls approximately five percent of the time.

21. Ibid., 28.

22. Ibid., 50. The Catholic Church has affirmed her belief in the inspiration of the additional material found in the Jeremiah and Samuel of the Masoretic Texts (as well as the Greek additions to the books of Daniel and Esther, found in the Septuagint, but not in the Masoretic Texts—but more on that in the next section).

rection. Some were tortured, refusing to accept release, that they might rise again to a better life" (11:35). The first half of the verse refers to the times when God used the prophets Elijah and Elisha to return dead children to their mothers (1 Kings 17:17–24; 2 Kings 4:25–37); but which OT example is the author appealing to in the second half?

It was an event recorded in 2 Maccabees 7:1–42. When the Seleucid king Antiochus IV desecrated the temple in 168 BC, he instituted an intense persecution of the Jews, forcing them to choose between martyrdom and violating the Mosaic Law. One mother watched as six of her sons, one after the other, chose death rather than apostasy, and as the time came for the seventh she encouraged him: "My son, have pity on me. I carried you nine months in my womb, and nursed you for three years, and have reared you and brought you up to this point in your life.... Do not fear this butcher, but prove worthy of your brothers. Accept death, so that in God's mercy I may get you back again with your brothers" (2 Macc. 7:27, 29).

If you have a Bible published by a Catholic or Eastern Orthodox publisher, you can easily flip to the story and read it in its entirety. If your copy of the Hebrew Scriptures was printed by a Jewish publisher, or a Protestant publisher following later Judaism's lead, then you will likely need to search elsewhere for the story. The Septuagint collection, used by the author of Hebrews, contained books that were not later included in the Masoretic Text, but continued in use among Christians.

These seven books are referred to as "deuterocanonical" by Catholics, and as "apocrypha" by Protestants. They are Tobit, Judith, Wisdom, Sirach, Baruch, 1 & 2 Maccabees, an additional 107 verses in the Book of Esther and two chapters in the Book of Daniel. At the time of Jesus and the apostles, there was no set Jewish "canon," or authoritative list, of Scripture[23]; but different groups within Judaism recognized different books as *sacred* ("soiling the hands" in rabbinic terminology). For instance, the Sadducees whom we read of in the gospels seem to have recognized nothing outside of the

---

23. *Canon* comes to us from the Greek term for a "rod" or "measuring stick."

Torah[24]—Genesis, Exodus, Leviticus, Numbers, and Deuteronomy—whereas the Pharisees seem to have recognized a group of texts corresponding largely, if not exactly, to those making up today's list of Hebrew Scriptures. The Essenes, the sect that preserved the Dead Sea Scrolls, made use of a much larger group of texts, including the deuterocanonicals Sirach and Tobit as well as works such as Jubilees and 1 Enoch.[25]

So how did Jews and Christians come to regard different books as Scripture? As I said, the Septuagint was the preferred version of the Hebrew Scriptures for the apostles and early Church, and the deuterocanonicals were included in this translation tradition. These books did not simply appear one day in connection with the other Old Testament texts; if the Church had them, it was because its earliest Jewish members brought these books *with them*.[26] Following the fall of Jerusalem, when Judaism's leading rabbis made a concerted effort to record their oral traditions in the Mishnah (ca. AD 200), they also appear to have definitively settled upon their canon.[27] In response, some Christian bishops and scholars, especially those in the east, began to feel that their Old Testament canon should reflect that of the Jews. Saint Jerome, who translated the Old and New Testaments from Hebrew and Greek into the Latin of the Roman Empire, felt this way. Doing his work as a translator in

24. This is thought to underlie the exchange between Jesus and the Pharisees in Mark 12:17–18.

25. Fragments of Tobit were found among the Dead Sea Scrolls in both Hebrew and Aramaic, and fragments of Sirach in Hebrew. Fragments from Sirach were also found in the ruins of Masada, the mountaintop Jewish fortification breached by the Romans in AD 73.

26. Albert C. Sunderberg Jr., "The Septuagint: The Bible of Hellenistic Judaism," in *The Canon Debate*, 80–90.

27. The reader is likely familiar with the frequently cited datum that the Jewish canon was declared closed by the rabbinic school in Jamnia (also seen as Yavneh/Jabneh) around AD 90. This has been completely disproven. The written records show that the rabbis discussed the canonical status of only two books—Ecclesiastes and the Song of Songs. The *suggestion* that the rabbis closed their canon at Jamnia was first made by Heinrich Graetz in 1871; but it was repeated so often that within a matter of decades it was asserted as a fact. I heartily recommend the essay by Jack P. Lewis, "Jamnia Revisited," in *The Canon Debate*, 146–162.

Bethlehem, alongside the rabbis of the late fourth century, Jerome became partial to their views regarding the deuterocanonicals, although in his writings he continued to quote from them as he did the other books of the OT. The Christian Church affirmed the deuterocanonicals as Scripture at the local council of Rome, presided over by Pope St. Damasus (AD 382), and again at the local councils of Hippo (AD 393) and Carthage (AD 419), the latter presided over by St. Augustine.[28] The deuterocanonicals continued to be used in the liturgy of the Church of both the east and west throughout the next millennium. The deuterocanonicals were included in the canon of the Scripture affirmed at the Ecumenical Council of Florence (AD 1442).[29]

The pope and bishops dogmatically reaffirmed the canon of the Old Testament at the Ecumenical Council of Trent (AD 1546). They did so then in response to Martin Luther's relegation of the deuterocanonicals to an appendix between the Old and New Testaments, and his labeling them "apocrypha." Luther and the other reformers turned to the rabbinic canon as the authority for their Old Testament. They wrongly assumed that the canon used by Medieval Judaism was more authentic, more original, than that used by the Catholics and Eastern Orthodox. As we saw above, the archaeological/literary findings of the past century do not bear this out.[30]

An objection Protestant commentators make to the apocrypha is that Jesus did not quote from them as he did from the rest of the Old Testament. The objection has a glaring flaw: If quotation from

28. Dr. John Bergsma, Associate Professor of Theology at the Franciscan University of Steubenville, has provided a chart illustrating the OT books recognized in the early Church: http://www.salvationhistory.com/documents/misc/Bergsma_Canon_Chart.pdf.

29. Session 11, *Bull of Union with the Copts.*

30. The Reformers also did not realize that the deuterocanonicals were not abandoned wholesale by Judaism. Sirach was quoted three times in the Talmud (ca. AD 400–500), and eighty-five citations of the book have been found in rabbinic literature up to the tenth century AD: Timothy Michael Law, *When God Spoke Greek*, 182, n. 15. There are likewise indications that Jews living in Spain in the twelfth and thirteenth centuries were familiar with Judith, as well as one of the additional stories found in Daniel (Bel and the Dragon): Albert C. Sunderberg Jr., *The Canon Debate*, 88.

Jesus or the apostles, as recorded in the New Testament, were the criterion for including books in the Old Testament, then all Christians would have to slim their Bibles, which would no longer contain Ecclesiastes, Obadiah, Zephaniah, Judges, 1 & 2 Chronicles, Ezra, Nehemiah, Lamentations, or Nahum.[31]

The deuterocanonicals may not be directly quoted from, but they were *certainly* paraphrased. Observe the way Sirach is employed by Jesus, and the Wisdom of Solomon by Paul[32]:

SIRACH 28:2

Forgive your neighbor the wrong he has done, and then your sins will be pardoned when you pray.

MATTHEW 6:14

For if you forgive men their trespasses, your heavenly Father also will forgive you.

Sirach 29:10–12

Lose your silver for the sake of a brother or a friend, and do not let it rust under a stone and be lost. Lay up your treasure according to the commandments of the Most High, and it will profit you more than gold. Store up almsgiving in your treasury, and it will rescue you from all affliction. . . .

LUKE 16:9

And I tell you, make friends for yourselves by means of unrighteous mammon [or money] so that when it fails they may receive you into the eternal habitations.

ROMANS 1:22–25

Claiming to be wise, they became fools, and exchanged the glory of the immortal God for images resembling mortal man or birds or animals or reptiles. Therefore, God gave them up in the lusts of their hearts to impurity, to the dishonoring of their bodies among themselves, because they exchanged the truth about God for a lie and worshiped and served the creature rather than the Creator.

WISDOM 12:24–25

For they went far astray on the paths of error, accepting as gods those animals which even their enemies despised; they were deceived like foolish infants. Therefore, as to thoughtless children, you sent your judgment to mock them.

---

31. Mark P. Shea, *By What Authority?: An Evangelical Discovers Catholic Tradition* (Huntington, IN: Our Sunday Visitor Inc., 1996), 62.

32. An extensive list of New Testament references to the deuterocanonical texts is available online at http://www.cin.org/users/james/files/deutero3.htm.

You may also recall how, when I discussed the Trinity in chapter one, I noted the way Hebrews 1:2–3 draws from Wisdom 7:25–27 in its description of Christ as the preexistent Son. As an interesting aside: John's Gospel (10:22–23) tells us that Jesus, like all Jews today, celebrated the feast of Hanukkah; yet this feast is not established in any book of the Jewish or Protestant Bibles. Rather, 1 Maccabees 4:52–59 is where we find the record of Hanukkah's establishment as an annual feast, in 164 BC.

Authoritative Oral Traditions

Hebrews also witnesses to the Catholic conviction that the Word of God communicates himself and his truth to us through more than just the written word. The revelations written down in the Old Testament, and appealed to by the author of Hebrews, began not as texts but as historical experiences of God and orally-delivered prophecies. The *Mishnah* recorded the Jewish belief that alongside the written Torah, there had always existed an oral body of truth— what later generations dubbed the "oral Torah." In the *Talmud* we read, "Moses received the Torah on Sinai, and handed it down to Joshua; Joshua to the Elders; the Elders to the Prophets; and the prophets handed it down to the men of the Great Assembly."[33] This oral body of truth grew as God continued to intervene in the life of Israel, and it was handed on to subsequent generations.

In chapter eleven the author of Hebrews seeks to strengthen his readers by citing numerous examples of faithful Israelites who had endured persecution and martyrdom in witness to God's truth. He reminds them how some were stoned, while others were "sawn in two. . . ." (Heb. 11:37). His Jewish readers would have recognized the latter as a reference to the martyrdom of the prophet Isaiah—an event not recorded in the OT, but handed down in oral tradition.[34] In an interesting parallel to this verse, in Matthew 23:35 we find

---

33. Mishnah-tractate *Avot* 1:1, quoted in Abraham Cohen, *Everyman's Talmud: The Major Teachings of the Rabbinic Sages* (New York: Schocken Books, 1995), xxxvi.
34. It was eventually recorded in *The Martyrdom of Isaiah*.

Jesus endorsing the oral tradition that Zechariah the prophet had been martyred in the temple.[35]

St. Paul appeals to Jewish tradition in his epistles as well. He recounts how the rock that miraculously gushed water when struck by Moses (Exod. 17:3–6) followed the Israelites throughout their wanderings in the desert (1 Cor. 10:4), a tradition that was later recorded in the Talmud.[36] In 2 Timothy 3:8, Paul warned the young bishop Timothy about the kind of men who would be plentiful in the last days, using the "Jannes and Jambres [who] opposed Moses" as examples of men of "corrupt mind and counterfeit faith." These names were passed down in Jewish tradition as the names of the Egyptian magicians who opposed Moses (Exod. 7:11; 9:11). You may also recall from chapter one how the author of Hebrews endorsed the Jewish tradition that Moses was given the Law not by God Himself, but through the mediation of angels (Heb. 2:2). Let us not forget that the inspiration of both our author and Paul vouchsafes the truth of these specific elements of oral tradition!

The Epistle of Jude may be the New Testament's strongest witness to tradition's ability to communicate revelation. Only one chapter in length, Jude mentions both the conflict between Satan and the Archangel Michael over the body of Moses, eventually recorded in *The Assumption of Moses*, and an authentic prophecy handed down through time and, prior to the birth of Christ, recorded in the Book of Enoch: "It was of these also that Enoch in the seventh generation from Adam prophesied, saying, 'Behold, the Lord came with myriads of his holy ones, to execute judgment on all, and to convict all the ungodly of their deeds of ungodliness. . . .'" (Jude 14–15; Book of Enoch 1:9).

Not only were elements of God's word handed down in Jewish tradition, but it was impossible to fully comprehend the written

---

35. This tradition was later recorded in the *Targum on Lamentations* 2, 20. Some mistakenly believe Jesus referred to the martyrdom of Zechariah the son of Jehoiada, narrated in 2 Chron. 24:20–22; but Matthew recorded Jesus speaking of "the son of Berachiah," one of the twelve minor prophets, whose martyrdom was a matter handed down not in Scripture, but tradition. Scott Hahn and Curtis Mitch, *The Ignatius Study Bible: New Testament* (San Francisco: Ignatius Press), 49.

36. Mishnah-tractates *Taanit* 9a and *Bava Metizia* 86b.

word without the tradition. Written Hebrew had no vowels (those were added by the Masoretes centuries later). You can imagine the number of words formed using the same sequence of consonants, and context cannot always assure the correct reading. (To give a modern example: Did you have *Coke* or *cake* with dinner last night?) Each generation that proclaimed the written word in the temple, synagogue, and scribal schools was dependent upon the preceding generation for the correct reading of the text![37]

Christian Tradition Conveys God's Revelation

We find Tradition serving an analogous function in Christianity. Look at how the author of the Epistle to the Hebrews presumes it:

> For though by this time you ought to be teachers, you need some one to teach you again the first principles of God's word.... Therefore let us leave the *elementary doctrines of Christ* and go on to maturity, not laying again a foundation of repentance from dead works and of faith toward God, with *instructions* about baptisms, the laying on of hands, the resurrection of the dead, and eternal judgment. And this we will do if God permits. (Heb. 5:12, 6:1–3)

According to Hebrews, baptism and the laying on of hands (confirmation)—the sacramental life of the Church—are among "the first principles of God's *word*."[38] And yet, the apostles did not write down these instructions but handed them on orally as part of what the Catholic Church calls Sacred Tradition.[39] That was the Great Com-

---

37. Law, *When God Spoke Greek*, 22–23.

38. N.T. Wright, *Hebrews for Everyone* (Louisville, KY: Westminster John Knox Press, 2004), 58.

39. You will note my capitalization of the word Tradition. This is standard practice in Catholicism, and is used to refer to the matters of *faith* and *morality* transmitted by Christ, through the Church. Tradition must be distinguished from *traditions*, customs and disciplines—such as abstaining from meat on Fridays, or women wearing head coverings during Mass—which, although spanning centuries, and having wonderful intents, remain *disciplines*, and not unchanging points of religious and moral truth. They are open to modification and outright suspension by the Church's ordained leaders. Blurring the line between Tradition and traditions often leads to needless, embarrassing arguments between Catholics, as well as between Catholics and non-Catholic Christians.

mission Christ gave the apostles: "Go therefore and make disciples of all nations, baptizing them in the name of the Father and of the Son and of the Holy Spirit, *teaching* them to observe *all that I have commanded you*; and behold, I am with you always, to the close of the age" (Matt. 28:19–20). When St. Paul wrote to the Thessalonians he instructed them to "stand firm and hold to the *traditions* which you were taught by us, *either by word of mouth* or by letter" (2 Thess. 2:15). Remember, Christianity is not a religion of the book, but of the Word—the Word "we have looked upon and touched with our hands" (1 John 1:1). The Word became flesh, and he communicates his truth not just through Scripture, but through Tradition— handed on from one generation to the next.[40]

It is no accident that the sacraments are a subject of much disagreement among the Christian communities that separated from the Catholic Church and rejected its claim to transmit apostolic Tradition. In rejecting this elementary aspect of God's word, and focusing solely on that which was committed to writing, they opened themselves up to countless disagreements; and tragically, they have no recourse for arriving at a solution. Consider baptism: Does the act *make us* children of God, or is it merely symbolic? Must candidates for baptism be fully immersed in water; or is it sufficient to pour it over the candidates' heads, or sprinkle it on them? May infants be baptized, or must a child wait until he or she has reached the "age of reason"? The answers to all of these questions—as well as so many other treasures God intends for His children—are there in Sacred Tradition, just waiting to be taken up and lived.

This Tradition, because it comes from the incarnate Word and the Spirit, is free of the errors for which Jesus excoriated the Pharisees (Matt. 15:7–9). This is what we refer to as the *infallibility* of the Church.[41] Christ told the apostles, "He who hears you hears *me*, and

---

40. Thus we read St. Paul's command to his young bishop, Timothy: "[W]hat you have heard from me before many witnesses entrust to faithful men who will be able to teach others also" (2 Tim. 2:2).

41. Because the Church has been charged with announcing Christ's truth to the world, he prevents her, in her official statements regarding faith and morals, from teaching anything false. We will discuss infallibility at greater length in chapter seven.

he who rejects you rejects me" (Lk. 10:16). Because of that, the Church is "the pillar and bulwark of truth" (1 Tim. 3:15). Her Sacred Tradition is the fulfillment, the completion, of Judaism's oral Torah.[42]

Without Tradition we would not have the collection of writings we call the New Testament. All of the texts were inspired and written during the days of the apostles, but hundreds of years passed before the Church gathered them between two covers. For the early Church the "New Testament," or "New Covenant," was the *Eucharist* (1 Cor. 11:25; Lk. 22:20); and what we now *call* the "New Testament" consisted of the texts used in the Church's worship, along with those of the OT.[43] If you consult the Appendix, you will see that the canon of the NT was slimmer in its initial stages; many documents that we now accept were once in doubt within certain quarters of the Church.[44] While all of the documents had been in existence since the time of the apostles, we have to remember that some of these may have taken time to reach distant areas—each document needed to be recopied by hand and then walked to its destination. With that type of transmission going on, the history and tradition backing various documents would have suffered in some locales. If we consider the matter fairly, we could not expect all bishops in different areas to be aware of how many epistles Peter or John had written— initially the bishops were probably only familiar with the writings that had been sent to their communities, or the ones closest to them. The Church had to begin a process of gaining knowledge of the claims attached to these books; and then its ordained leaders used the charism of truth, bequeathed to them by the apostles,[45] to recognize which books issued from the Holy Spirit.

Before the Word ever found expression in writing, it already existed fully within the Church (Jude 3). God never meant for "the

---

42. Lawrence Feingold, *The Mystery of Israel and the Church, Vol. III: The Messianic Kingdom of Israel* (St. Louis: The Miriam Press, 2010), 120.

43. Scott Hahn, *Consuming the Word: The New Testament and the Eucharist in the Early Church* (New York: Image, 2013), 10.

44. This was true for the Epistle to the Hebrews.

45. Again, more on this in chapter seven.

Book" to make either Tradition or the Church's role as teacher obsolete. If he had, then he would have made sure the printing press was invented before the fifteenth century. He also would have seen to it that more than just the upper crust of society was taught to read prior to last century. Truth is trinitarian. The One God exists as a three-fold, reciprocal relationship of love; and the fullness of His truth is guaranteed to us through the reciprocal relationship existing between Scripture, Tradition, and the teaching office of the Church.

Catholic Truth

"Catholic" comes from the Greek word *katholikos*, meaning "universal; all-embracing." First witnessed to in writing in AD 107, in the letters of Ignatius of Antioch, "catholic" was the ideal adjective to describe Christ's Church, reaching out to gather Jew and every manner of Gentile into one Body. It also captures the Church's stance toward God's word: *We want all of it*—the *whole* truth! We want Scripture—the Old Testament (*all 46 books* used by the early Church) and the New. We want the Tradition Christ delivered to the apostles. We want the fullness of the truth, the Word made flesh, himself, as he gives himself and his supernatural life to us in the sacraments.

Once we come to believe that God addresses us through Scripture and Tradition, we are duty bound to seek these two things out and begin living them. Jesus was adamant: "Not every one who says to me, 'Lord, Lord,' shall enter the kingdom of heaven, but he who does the will of my Father who is in heaven" (Matt. 7:21); "If you love me, you will keep my commandments" (John 14:15). And as the writer of the Epistle to the Hebrews reminded his readers—and us today—deliberately turning our backs on the God who loved us enough to become man to bring about our salvation, and adamantly refusing to live in His friendship, has terrifying consequences:

> For it is impossible to restore again to repentance those who have once been enlightened, who have tasted the heavenly gift, and have become partakers of the Holy Spirit, and have *tasted the goodness*

of the word of God and the powers of the age to come, if they then commit apostasy, since they crucify the Son of God on their own account and hold him up to contempt. . . . Though we speak thus, yet in your case, beloved, we feel sure of better things that belong to salvation. (Heb. 6:4–6, 9)[46]

46. Notice again how the word of God is linked to the sacramental life of the Church: "once been *enlightened*" (early Christians referred to baptism as "enlightenment"); "tasted the heavenly gift" (the Eucharist? see John 6:30–71); "become partakers of the Holy Spirit" (which comes to perfection in confirmation—see Acts 8:14–17).

4

Christ's Priesthood, Our Salvation

HEBREWS, CHAPTERS 7–11

*[Christ] has appeared once for all at the end of the age to put away
sin by the sacrifice of himself.* ⁓*Hebrews 9:26*

*Therefore do not throw away your confidence, which has a great
reward. For you have need of endurance, so that you may do the will
of God and receive what is promised.* ⁓*Hebrews 10:35–36*

In this chapter we will explore the way Christ, high priest in the
order of Melchizedek, saves us from sin. We will begin by seeing
how the author of Hebrews presents Jesus' death, Resurrection, and
ascension as the fulfillment of Judaism's Temple sacrifices, and most
especially of Yom Kippur, the Day of Atonement. With that as a
foundation we will then examine the Catholic Church's understanding of the way the salvation won for us by Christ becomes ours
through faith, baptism, and a life spent "abiding" in Christ.

The Earthly Temple Gives Way to the Heavenly

As we have said, the original recipients of the Epistle to the Hebrews
were under tremendous pressure to abandon their faith in Christ as
the Messiah and return to the more "mainstream" expression of
Judaism into which they had been born. Our author had to remind
them that doing so would have been a rejection of the new and
more excellent covenant foretold by the prophets. The Old Covenant and its worship were good, but they only foreshadowed the
greater reality that took flesh in Christ:

> In speaking of a new covenant [God, through the prophet Jere-
> miah,] treats the first [covenant] as obsolete. And what is becom-

ing obsolete and growing old is ready to vanish away. Now even the first covenant had regulations for worship and an earthly sanctuary. For a tent was prepared, the outer one, in which were the lampstand and the table and the bread of offering; it is called the Holy Place. Behind the second curtain stood a tent called the Holy of Holies, having the golden altar of incense and the ark of the covenant covered on all sides with gold . . . above it were the cherubim of glory overshadowing the mercy seat. Of these things we cannot now speak in detail. (Heb. 8:13–9:5)

The author of Hebrews was able to take his audience's knowledge of these things for granted, but we today could benefit from at least a little background knowledge.[1]

When Israel was in the desert, after it had received the Ten Commandments, God gave Moses detailed instructions for creating a portable sanctuary (Exod. 25:9, 40). Once Israel was settled into the Holy Land that sanctuary was translated into stone by David and Solomon—the Temple in Jerusalem.[2] The Jewish people knew that the Creator of the universe could not be contained in a tent or building (1 Kings 8:27). Nevertheless, the Tabernacle (tent in the desert) and Temple were heaven's embassy on earth, *the place* where the utterly transcendent God came to meet His people. God commanded the Israelites to come there in pilgrimage three times a year, and it was the sole place from which he would accept their sacrifices—the very heart of Israelite worship.[3]

When reading Hebrews you notice that the author constantly refers back to the Tabernacle that was packed up and unpacked throughout Israel's forty years in the desert. By doing so he high-

---

1. For a more in-depth treatment of the Temple's significance and the daily liturgy, as well as its meaning for today's Christian, I refer you to my book *Through, With, and In Him: The Prayer Life of Jesus and How to Make It Our Own* (Kettering, OH: Angelico Press, 2014), 8–26.

2. The Temple was destroyed by the Babylonians in 586 BC.; rebuilt when the Jews returned from the Babylonian Exile several decades later; desecrated by the Seleucids but rededicated by the Maccabees in 164 BC.; and made the recipient of a forty-six year enrichment and expansion project under Herod the Great. The Temple was, as prophesied by Christ, subsequently destroyed by the Romans in AD 70. Islam's Dome of the Rock has stood on the site for over thirteen hundred years.

3. See Exod. 23:14–17, 34:22–23; and Deut. 12:13–14.

lights the transitory nature of the institution. (Jerusalem's richly ornate, stone Temple proffered the illusion of permanence.) Both the Tabernacle and Temple had an enclosed courtyard where sacrificial animals were washed, killed, and placed upon the altar, as well as an "outer" and an "inner" sanctuary, the Holy Place and Holy of Holies respectively, separated from one another by a thick veil. The Holy of Holies was God's earthly throne room. For hundreds of years it was the resting place of the Ark of the Covenant, the golden chest containing the tablets with the Ten Commandments. On its lid were two golden cherubim, angels, with outstretched wings; above them, God was said to sit "enthroned" (Ps. 80:1, 99:1; 2 Kings 19:15).[4]

Even though Israel was a priestly people (Exod. 19:6), only a relatively small number of Israelites ever came near the sacrificial altar or entered the Temple's interior. Only one of Israel's twelve tribes, the Levites, were eligible to serve in the Temple; and only those descended from Moses' brother Aaron could be ordained as priests. The Temple consisted of a system of courts, with ever-stricter rules as to who could proceed farther into its heart: Gentiles could not advance past the first court, nor could Israelite women go past the second, or Israelite men past the third. Although priests ministered in the courtyard of sacrifice and the Holy Place, they were barred from the Holy of Holies. Only the high priest entered the Holy of Holies, the Temple's most sacred area; and he only did so once a year, on the feast of Yom Kippur. In hindsight we Christians understand the Temple's courts and restrictions as a representation of the way sin divided the members of the human family from one another and separated our entire race from God.

The Levitical priests acted as their brothers' and sisters' representatives before God. Each day at nine o'clock in the morning and three o'clock in the afternoon, a group of priests placed the perpetual offering, the *tamid*, on the altar—a lamb, cake of bread, and wine (Exod. 29:38–41). As they did so, another priest ascended the staircase from the court of the priests to enter the Holy Place—a room overlaid in pure gold and illuminated by the menorah, the

---

4. The Ark disappeared at the time of the Babylonian Exile in 586 BC. Even when empty, however, the Holy of Holies continued to be sacred.

seven-branched lamp. He passed a table holding twelve loaves of showbread to burn incense on a small altar before the veil leading to the Holy of Holies.

Between the morning and afternoon *tamid* the priests were in constant motion offering their brothers' and sisters' individual sacrifices upon the altar. Israelites offered sacrifices to seek forgiveness of sins, praise God's magnificence, acknowledge his bounty, and give thanks for his help. One specific form of thanksgiving sacrifice, the *todah*, or sacrifice of praise, was required of those whom God had saved from life-threatening crises. In the *todah*, as in other offerings, a portion of the animal was offered to God by fire, a second portion held back to be eaten by the priests, and a third portion consumed by the offerer and his family in a celebratory feast. In this way God and His people were united in the life of the sacrificial victim; communion was established, and the laity were made "partners in the altar" (1 Cor. 10:18).

We today, in a largely urban society, are mystified as to why God would ask for animal sacrifices. The Israelites, though, were people of the land. They either raised their own food or lived just down a dirt path from the people from whom they purchased it. Ultimately, sacrifice was not about spilling blood. When God asked them to sacrifice animals from their flocks, or a portion of their produce, bread, and wine, He asked them, in a very literal way, to share their *lives* with Him (Lev. 17:11, 23:18; Exod. 29:38–42). In hindsight we recognize that God was revealing what it means to be His sons and daughters—to image the Son in offering back to the Father all that we have received, our very selves. Under the Old Covenant it occurred in a veiled way.

The Day of Atonement

This is the lesson the author of the Epistle to the Hebrews drove home to his readers—especially the way that Christ's sacrifice fulfilled the offering made on the high holy day of *Yom Kippur.* "[I]nto the [Holy of Holies] only the high priest goes, and he but once a year, and not without taking blood which he offers for himself and for the errors of the people" (Heb. 9:7). The high priest atoned for the sins of the nation by sacrificing a bull and a goat. He carried their blood with him into the Holy Place, and only after sprinkling the blood, *the life*, on the great veil did he dare to enter the Holy of Holies. Once inside he sprinkled the blood on the Ark of the Covenant, both to atone for sin and to purify the Temple.[5] The author of Hebrews reminded his readers that the Levitical priests "serve[d] a copy and shadow of the heavenly sanctuary," modeled after "the pattern which was shown [to Moses]" (Heb. 8:5). And just as the Temple was but a shadow of a greater reality, so too were its sacrifices:

> [S]ince the law has but a shadow of the good things to come instead of the true form of these realities, it can never, by the same sacrifices which are continually offered year after year, make perfect those who draw near. Otherwise, would they not have ceased to be offered? If the worshipers had once been cleansed, they would no longer have any consciousness of sin. But in these sacrifices there is a reminder of sin year after year. For it is impossible that the blood of bulls and goats should take away sins. Consequently, when Christ came into the world, he said, "Sacrifices and offerings you have not desired, / but a body have you prepared for me; / in burnt offerings and sin offerings you have taken no pleasure. / Then I said, 'Behold, I have come to do your will, O God,' / as it is written of me in the roll of the book." (Heb. 10:1–7)

Jesus, and the perfect gift he made of himself to the Father—from the first instant of his conception all the way through to his death, Resurrection, and ascension into heaven—is the reality to which the shadows pointed. It was Jesus's sacrifice, cutting through time and space (Heb. 9:26; Rev. 13:8), that actually took away sins committed under the Mosaic Covenant:

> [W]hen Christ came as high priest of the good things that have come to be, passing through the greater and more perfect tabernacle not made by hands, that is, not belonging to this creation, he entered once for all into the sanctuary, not with the blood of goats and calves but with his own blood, thus obtaining eternal redemption. For if the blood of goats and bulls and the sprinkling of a heifer's ashes can sanctify those who are defiled so that their flesh

---

5. Since the disappearance of the Ark in 586 BC, the high priest had sprinkled the blood on the spot where the Ark had stood.

is cleansed, how much more will the blood of Christ, who through the eternal spirit offered himself unblemished to God, cleanse our consciences from dead works to worship the living God. (Heb. 9:11–14)[6]

The author of Hebrews reminded his readers—who were under extreme pressure to forsake Christ and return to the sacrificial system of the Old Covenant—that, because the fulfillment had come, the shadow would soon "vanish away" (Heb. 8:13). His claim was corroborated not just by the destruction of the Temple in AD 70, but by rabbinic tradition surrounding *Yom Kippur*.

Two different tracts of the *Babylonian Talmud* tell of the scarlet thread used in the *Yom Kippur* liturgy. It was a visible manifestation of God's promise that "though your sins are like scarlet, they shall be as white as snow; though they are red like crimson, they shall become like wool" (Isa. 1:18). The rabbis taught:

> At first [on the Day of Atonement, after the high priest performed his special worship], they would tie a crimson thread to the outside of the door of the [Temple] entrance-way. [If] it turned white, [the people] would rejoice; [if] it did not turn white, [the people] would be grieved.... For *forty years prior* to the destruction of the Temple, the crimson thread did not turn white, but rather remained red.[7]

The significance of the forty years is that the miracle ceased at the time of Christ's death, in approximately AD 30.[8] Recall how at Christ's death the veil cordoning off the Holy of Holies was torn in two, from top to bottom (Matt. 27:51). It was God the Father's announcement that the sacrifice and liturgy of Yom Kippur had been completed: Jesus's life-blood poured out upon the Cross parted the "veil" separating God and man; and at his ascension into

---

6. *New American Bible*, revised edition.

7. Tractate Rosh Hashanah 31b, in Jacob Neusner, *The Babylonian Talmud: A Translation and Commentary*, vol. 6, *Tractate Besah. Tractate Rosh Hashanah* (Peabody, MA: Hendrickson Publishers, 2005), 195–96, quoted in Lawrence Feingold, *The Mystery of Israel and the Church, Vol. I: Figure and Fulfillment* (St. Louis: The Miriam Press, 2010), 128.

8. John P. Meier, *A Marginal Jew*, 401–6.

heaven Jesus offered back to the Father the new life he had received in the Resurrection.[9] Jesus, the representative head of our race, made atonement for us by his obedience unto death; and with his bodily entrance into glory, a member of the human race had finally achieved the end for which we were created. Jesus now acts as our high priest, our perpetual intercessor with the Father. All that remains is for his victory to be appropriated to his brothers and sisters.

A Priest in the Order of Melchizedek

In Christ, God established a priesthood superior to that of the Levites. The writer of Hebrews was not surprised by this, since it had been prophesied by King David a thousand years before: "The LORD says to my lord: / 'Sit at my right hand, / till I make your enemies your footstool.' / . . . The LORD has sworn and will not change his mind, / 'You are a priest for ever according to the order of Melchizedek'" (Ps. 110:1, 4).

Melchizedek was a mysterious figure. We catch only the briefest glimpse of him in Genesis. He abruptly appears in the narrative while Abraham, the father of the Jews, is returning from a military victory over a vastly superior force. Melchizedek, identified as a "priest of God Most High" and king of Salem, offered a thanksgiving sacrifice (*todah*) on Abraham's behalf—bread and wine—with the prayer, "Blessed be Abram by God Most High, maker of heaven and earth; and blessed be God Most High, who has delivered your enemies into your hand!" (Gen. 14:19–20).

Psalm 110, where David writes of a priest in the order of Melchizedek, was widely recognized as messianic.[10] The Messiah, coming from the line of David (of the tribe of Judah), would be both priest and king, as Melchizedek had been over a millennium before. Levitical priests became qualified for service upon demonstration of their priestly lineage. Melchizedek had no such docu-

---

9. Recall how in the Septuagint, the Greek term used by the author of Hebrews to describe Christ's resurrected humanity, *teleiō*, was used in reference to priestly ordination—the role Christ exercised in his Paschal Mystery.

10. Christ spoke of it as such (Matt. 22:44–45).

mentation, yet Abraham reverenced him as one greater than himself; thus, his priesthood was superior to the Levites' (Heb. 7:4–11). Melchizedek disappeared from the narrative of Genesis just as abruptly as he came, with Scripture containing no record of his death. Hebrews' author saw this as pointing ahead to the eternal nature of Christ' priesthood:

> [Jesus became] a priest, not according to a legal requirement concerning bodily descent [from Levi] but by the power of an indestructible life. . . . The former priests were many because they were prevented by death from continuing in office; but he holds his priesthood permanently, because he continues for ever. Consequently he is able for all time to save those who draw near to God through him, since he always lives to make intercession for them. For it was fitting that we should have such a high priest, holy, blameless, unstained, separated from sinners, exalted above the heavens. He has no need, like [Levitical] high priests, to offer sacrifices daily, first for his own sins and then for those of the people; he did this once for all when he offered up himself. Indeed, the law appoints men in their weakness as high priests, but the word of the oath, which came later than the law, appoints a Son who has been made perfect for ever. (Heb. 7:16, 23–28)

The New Covenant

Because the Levitical priesthood was mandated by the Law of Moses, the introduction of a new priesthood—Christ's in the order of Melchizedek—meant there had to be a corresponding change of law (Heb. 7:12). Although the Levitical priesthood and the Mosaic Law were holy in and of themselves, they lacked the power to reach inside men and women to undo the damage wrought by sin (Rom. 7:7–25). A more powerful remedy was needed; and just as the OT Scriptures had prophesied a new priesthood, so too there would be a new covenant:

> Christ has obtained a ministry which is as much more excellent than the [Levitical] as the covenant he mediates is better, since it is enacted on better promises. For if that first covenant had been faultless, there would have been no occasion for a second. For [God] finds fault with them when he says [through Jeremiah the prophet]: "The days will come, says the Lord, when I will establish

a new covenant with the house of Israel and with the house of Judah; not like the covenant that I made with their fathers.... *I will put my laws into their minds, and write them on their hearts,* and I will be their God ... all shall know me, from the least of them to the greatest. For I will be merciful toward their iniquities, and I will remember their sins no more." (Heb. 8:6–12; Jer. 31:31–34)

The new covenant that God offers far surpasses the old. In Christ we are not only told the right way to go; we are transformed from fallen creatures into sons and daughters, and given divine power to live in God's image. This was the salvation longed for by Jew and Gentile; and in Jesus it was offered to both, independent of the Law and Temple sacrifices.

No Longer Under the Torah

We have to try to understand the friction such a proclamation caused between Jewish Christians and their families—not to mention the high priest and elders. Obedience to the Law, the Torah, was what had set the Jews apart as God's chosen people; it *defined* them. Did faith in Christ entail its repudiation?

That certainly was not Jesus's intent. "Do not think that I have come to abolish the law and the prophets; I have come *not to abolish* them but to *fulfil* them" (Matt. 5:17). That was how the early Church understood Christ's life and passage to the Father and the sacraments: Jesus's body was the definitive Temple in which God dwelt— both his physical body (John 2:19–21) and his mystical body, the Church (Eph. 1:22–23, 2:21–22); the Saturday Sabbath became Sunday, the Lord [Jesus]'s Day (Acts 20:7; Rev. 1:3); the *tamid* and *Yom Kippur* found their fulfilment in Jesus' death, resurrection, and ascension; the rite of circumcision in baptism (Col. 2:11–12); the Passover in the Eucharist (1 Cor. 5:7–8, 11:23–25)—as did the *todah* and *tamid*. The Torah was not abolished, but fulfilled and transformed—as was Jesus' own Torah-observant humanity in the Resurrection!

Sadly, the majority of Jewish people who heard the message misinterpreted it. Fulfilment was misconstrued as abolishment. We see this when the deacon Stephen was led before the Sanhedrin. His accusers charged him with speaking against the Temple and Law: "we have heard him say that this Jesus of Nazareth will destroy this place, and will change the customs which Moses delivered to us" (Acts 6:13–14). Everything hinges on how one understands "change." Was it "change" as when a boy grows into a man, or "change" as when a body is turned to ash? The early Church obviously believed it be the former (Gal. 3:23–29); but the majority of Jewish people, the latter.

Even within the early Church there was significant misunderstanding—albeit in the opposite direction. When Gentiles were admitted to the Christian community, an influential group of Jewish Christians insisted that the Gentiles begin living by all the Torah's prescriptions: circumcision, dietary restrictions, observance of feast days, etc. It caused tremendous turmoil, with Gentiles being reluctant to take on such stringent stipulations; and, as a result, being looked upon as second-class citizens in the Church.

The resolution of this matter was the subject of the first Church council. The principle discerned and promulgated by the apostles was that both Jews and Gentiles were brought into a *saving* relationship with God not through the Torah, but *through the grace of Christ*; and therefore, the Gentiles should not be saddled with a burden that the Jews themselves had been unable to successfully bear (Acts 15:10–11). Even though that was the teaching of the council, a significant number of Jewish Christians (who came to be known as the "circumcision party")[11] still felt compelled to observe the Torah and sought to make it compulsory for Gentile Christians.

Paul addressed their error in a number of epistles. He insisted that the outward performance of the "works of the Law" (or "works of the Torah") did not make one interiorly holy in God's sight (Rom. 3:20, 28; Gal. 2:16; 3:2, 5, 10). Paul's phrase "works of the Law" also appears in the Dead Sea Scrolls. In the work *Misqat ma'ase ha-Torah* (*Some Works of the Torah*), the phrase was used to designate ceremonial precepts. [12] Paul used the term when discussing ceremo-

---

11. Galatians 2:12.

12. This work has also been called the *Sectarian Manifesto* and *Halakhic Letter*. Scholars often designate it 4QMMT. The text can be found in Michael Wise, Martin Abegg, Jr., and Edward Cook, *The Dead Sea Scrolls: A New Translation* (New York: Harper Collins Publishers, 1995), 358–64.

nial matters such as feast days (Gal. 4:10), clean and unclean foods (Gal. 2:12–13), and the work of Torah par excellence, circumcision (Rom. 4:9–12; Gal. 5:11–12). [13]

Because the Torah was a unified whole, Christ had done more than bring its ceremonial precepts to fulfillment; he completed the Law in its entirety. [14] Not only had Christ, as our representative, flawlessly met the demands of the Torah; he even took upon himself the curse that the Torah pronounced on those who broke the covenant. "Christ redeemed us from the curse of the law, having become a curse for us—for it is written, 'Cursed be every one who hangs on a tree'" (Gal. 3:13; Dt. 21:23). The Torah was a tutor, a disciplinarian meant to lead the Jewish people to Christ; and now that he had come both they and the Gentiles were meant to reap the benefits (Gal. 3:23–25). Unlike the rites, or "sacraments," of the Torah, the sacraments instituted by Christ are conduits of his own indestructible life: "As many of you as were *baptized into Christ* have put on Christ. There is neither Jew nor Greek, there is neither slave nor free, there is neither male nor female; for all you all are one in Christ Jesus" (Gal. 3:27–28). Just as the veil closing off the Holy of Holies was destroyed by Christ's death, so too were the Temple walls that divided Jew from Gentile and woman from man destroyed (Eph. 2:14).

Tragically, Paul's teaching that we have been freed from "works of the Law" led to later divisions among Christians. In the sixteenth century, Luther and others argued that a Christian's good works were of no value in attaining salvation. Luther was adamant that St. Paul taught we are saved by "faith alone." [15] St. Peter, in his second epistle, was inspired to praise Paul's writings; but he also urged caution upon readers: "Paul wrote to you according to the wisdom given him. . . . There are some things in [his letters that are] hard to

13. James Akin, *The Salvation Controversy* (El Cajon, CA: Catholic Answers Press, 2001), 97–98.

14. Ibid., 99.

15. Luther was so convinced in his understanding that, when translating Romans 3:28 from Greek into German, he sought to clarify Paul's thought by adding the word "alone" to the text: "For we hold that a man is justified by faith *alone* apart from works of law."

understand, which the ignorant and unstable twist to their own destruction" (2 Pet. 3:15–16).

This is never more true than when one tries to parse the distinction in Paul's writing between unnecessary "works of the Law" and other "works" that Paul taught *were*, in fact, necessary for salvation. In Romans, Paul's most extensive writing on the Christian's freedom from the works of the Law, he states clearly at the outset:

> [God] will render to every man according to his *works*: to those who by patience in *well-doing* seek for glory and honor and immortality, *he will give eternal life.* . . . it is not the hearers of the law who are righteous before God, but the doers of the law who will be justified. When Gentiles who have not the law do by nature what the law requires, they are a law to themselves, even though they do not have the law. They show that what the law requires is *written on their hearts*, while their conscience also bears witness and their conflicting thoughts accuse or perhaps excuse them on that day when, according to my gospel, God judges the secrets of men by Christ Jesus. (Rom. 2:6–7, 13–16)

Like Jewish believers, Gentile Christians also partook of the new covenant prophesied by Jeremiah, in which God "put [his] laws into their minds, and [wrote] them on their hearts" (Heb. 8:10).

Christians—Jews and Gentiles—are bound to *a law*, but it is not the Torah. Rather, it is the "Law of Christ" (Gal. 6:2; 1 Cor. 9:21). A significant portion of Christ's law is God's eternal law, or what philosophers and theologians call natural law. The tenets of the natural law are discernible by reason and incumbent upon every human conscience.[16] We find its prohibitions reflected across cultures (the condemnation of murder, adultery, treason, theft), although because of sin's power to distort the intellect, aberrations appeared (e.g., acceptance of polygamy, infanticide, euthanasia). To counter such errors, God explicitly reiterated the main precepts of the natural law in the Torah, in the Ten Commandments.[17] We Christians

---

16. Ibid., 103.
17. With the exception of the command to keep holy, specifically, the Sabbath day.

must live by these commands if we are to inherit eternal life. We are bound to them, however, not because they appear in the Torah; but because they are part of God's eternal law.[18] Paul said that he labored among the Gentiles to "bring about the *obedience* of faith" (Rom. 1:5). The Law of Christ also consists of Christ's positive commands: we must be baptized (Matt. 28:19; Mark 16:16), celebrate the Eucharist (Luke 22:19–20; John 6:43-54), and obey the shepherds of his Church (Luke 10:16; Matt. 18:18, 28:20; Heb. 13:17).[19] Jesus told the Apostles, "If you love me, you will *keep my commandments*" (John 14:15).

In actuality, the Law of Christ is far more demanding than the Torah's 613 commands. "A new commandment I give to you, that you love one another, even as I have loved you" (John 13:34). We are to refrain not just from adultery, but from even *looking lustfully* at members of the opposite sex (Matt. 5:28). Christ means to bring about a complete interior transformation. His goal is plainly stated: "You, therefore, *must be perfect*, as your heavenly Father is perfect" (Matt. 5:48). Christ would not call us to an impossible ideal. He is the Son of God, with the power to make his words reality (Matt. 19:26).

The Plan of Salvation [20]

In the last chapter we read the statement by the author of Hebrews that he did not intend to retrace the "elementary doctrines of Christ" by addressing "repentance from dead works and of faith toward God, with instruction about baptisms, the laying on of hands, the resurrection of the dead, and eternal judgment" (Heb. 6:1–2). And while he remained true to his word, I would argue that he still managed to give the New Testament's most thorough statement as to how we are saved, or "justified." Immediately after quoting Jeremiah's prophecy of the new covenant, he writes:

---

18. Ibid.

19. James Akin, *The Drama of Salvation: How God Rescues You From Sin and Brings You to Eternal Life* (El Cajon, CA: Catholic Answers Press, 2015), 112.

20. Adapted from Kapler, *The God Who is Love*, 93–101.

Therefore, brethren, since we have confidence to enter the [heavenly] sanctuary by the blood of Jesus, by the new and living way which he opened for us through the curtain, that is through his flesh, and since we have a great high priest over the house of God, let us draw near with a true heart in full assurance of faith, with our hearts sprinkled clean from an evil conscience and our bodies washed with pure water. Let us hold fast the confession of our hope without wavering, for he who promised is faithful; and let us consider how to stir up one another to love and good works, not neglecting to meet together, as is the habit of some, but encouraging one another, and all the more as you see the Day drawing near. (Heb. 10:19–23)

Faith is the beginning and foundation of our life in Christ. Hebrews defines it as "the assurance of things hoped for, the conviction of things not seen," and tells us that "without faith it is impossible to please" God (11:1, 6). Recognizing Jesus as God's Son and Messiah is the direct result of God's grace. Faith is a gift sown in our hearts by the Holy Spirit (Matt. 16:17; 1 Cor. 12:3). It is not blind belief. Rather, God assists the human intellect as it examines external proofs—such as the fulfillment of prophecy and the miracles of Christ and the apostles—and reaches the conclusion that Jesus is exactly who he and the Church claimed. This belief is but the beginning of our salvation: "to all who received him, who believed in his name, [Jesus] gave power to *become* children of God" (John 1:12). Faith comes to fruition when we turn away from sin (Mk. 1:15) and are baptized. Baptism is the *act* of faith.

As I said previously, the rites of the Old Law could only point ahead toward Christ, but the rites of the New actually communicate his life to us. As the waters of baptism wash over us, our sins are washed away and the Holy Spirit rushes into our souls, uniting us to Jesus. We become sons and daughters *in the Son*, participating in his relationship with the Father. Our souls share his conception by the power of the Spirit, and we are "born anew, not of perishable seed but of imperishable" (1 Pet. 1:23). We receive what later theologians called "sanctifying grace,"[21] and are made "partakers of the divine

---

21. CCC 1999–2000.

nature" (2 Pet. 1:4). Christ and the apostles were clear about baptism's efficacious nature.[22] Baptism is the way—through absolutely no merit on our part—that the effects of Christ's death and resurrection are first applied to our souls:

> We were therefore buried with him by baptism into death, so that as Christ was raised from the dead by the glory of the Father, we too might walk in newness of life. For if we have been united with him in a death like his, we shall certainly be united with him in a resurrection like his. (Rom. 6:3–5)

Baptism is also where Christians make their formal confession of faith.[23] In a reversal of the original sin, we reject Satan and his empty promises and profess our faith in the Father, Son, and Spirit. We do this by expressing our agreement with the Apostles' Creed. If we were brought to the sacrament as infants, then our parents expressed agreement in our names—reflections of Joseph and Mary having Jesus circumcised and made a member of the covenant people. Just as circumcision, performed when Jesus was eight days old, brought him into God's covenant and the religious community of Israel, so baptism brings us—even as infants—into the New Covenant and makes us members of Christ's mystical body, the Church (Acts 2:38–39). Physical circumcision is no longer required because, as St. Paul taught, baptism cuts away the carnal, sinful desires from our hearts (Col. 2:11–13; Rom. 2:26–29). It wipes away original sin and gives us the grace to overcome its effects. It fulfils Jeremiah's prophecy of the New Covenant as well as its parallel in Ezekiel, "I

---

22. "Truly, truly, I say to you, unless one is born of water and the Spirit, he cannot enter the kingdom of God" (John 3:5).

"[God] waited in the days of Noah, during the building of the ark, in which a few, that is, eight persons, were saved through the water. Baptism, which corresponds to this now saves you. . . ." (1 Pet. 3:20–21).

"[W]hen the goodness and loving kindness of God our Savior appeared, he saved us, not because of deeds done by us in righteousness, but in virtue of his own mercy, by the washing of regeneration and renewal in the Holy Spirit, which he poured out upon us richly through Jesus Christ our Savior, so that we might be justified by his grace and become heirs in hope of eternal life" (Titus 3:4–7).

23. We see how integral such a confession was to justification in the mind of Paul in Romans 10:9 and 1 Timothy 6:12.

will sprinkle clean water upon you, and you shall be clean. . . . And I will take out of your flesh the heart of stone and give you a heart of flesh. I will put my spirit within you and cause you to walk in my statutes" (Ezek. 36:25–27).

Through the Spirit, Jesus sets about reproducing his life within us. All of his actions during his time on earth were expressions of love for the Father, and as such they were performed in the power of the Holy Spirit. When he acts in us the same is true; Jesus is now loving the Father, in the Spirit, through us (Galatians 2:20–21). In baptism we were born anew, but God has no intention of letting us remain spiritual infants (Eph. 4:13; Heb. 6:1). He looks forward eagerly to our growth and development, and that means manifesting Christ in our actions. *United to our high priest*, we offer our bodily lives as "living sacrifice[s], holy and acceptable to God" (Rom. 12:1). The love of God, poured into our hearts by the Spirit (Rom. 5:5), propels us forward, moving us not just to listen to God's word but to put it into practice (James 1:22–25). Catholics call this "sanctification" or the "ongoing process of justification," recognizing birth and the subsequent process of growth as stages in *one and the same life*.

We are meant to be branches living by the life of the Vine, parts of the Body of which Jesus is the Head. If our lives are not showing forth His life, and progressively more so over the years, then something is wrong. "As the branch cannot bear fruit by itself, unless it abides in the vine, neither can you, unless you abide in me. . . . I am the true vine, and my Father is the vinedresser. Every branch of mine that bears no fruit, he takes away" (John 15:4, 1–2).

Final justification—when our souls will fully share the life of heaven—is not a matter of faith alone, but of faith and works. "For we are [God's] workmanship, created in Christ Jesus *for* good works, which God prepared beforehand, that we should walk in them" (Eph. 2:10). The most important thing to understand, though, is that the good works a Christian performs are never the Christian's alone—they are *primarily* the work of Christ himself. "[W]ork out your own salvation with fear and trembling; for God is at work in you, both to *will* and to *work* for his good pleasure" (Phil. 2:12–13). The action *originates* in Jesus but is *actualized* in us. The power to carry it out flows from the Holy Spirit; but the action does not occur without our "yes" and our active cooperation. And God the Father is truly pleased by that cooperation—like any father looking at the work his child "helped" him accomplish (even though it required the father to exert more energy than he would have had he simply done it himself). [24] God goes even further and "rewards" us with progressively more of his grace until, when, on the Day of Judgment, Christ raises us from the dead and bestows the crown of life.[25]

We "merit" this increase of grace; but, make no mistake, it is not in the legal sense of God owing us a payment for our work. On the contrary, we merit in the same way a child who eats everything on his plate merits a second helping; the merit is founded on the

24. "Now may the God of peace ... equip you with everything good that you may do his will, working in you that which is pleasing in his sight, through Jesus Christ, to whom be glory for ever and ever" (Heb. 13:20–21).

"In [Jesus], according to the purpose of him who accomplishes all things according to the counsel of his will, we who first hoped in Christ have been destined and appointed to live for the praise of his glory" (Eph. 1:11–12).

"I have received ... the gifts you sent, a fragrant offering, a sacrifice acceptable and pleasing to God" (Phil. 4:18). See also Phil 1:9–11; Col. 3:20; 2 Cor. 5:9–10; Rom. 12:1; 1 Tim. 2:1, 3; 1 John 3:21–22.

25. "His divine power has granted to us all things that pertain to life and godliness ... make every effort to supplement your faith with virtue, and virtue with knowledge, and knowledge with self-control, and self-control with steadfastness, and steadfastness with godliness, and godliness with brotherly affection, and brotherly affection with love. For *if* these things are yours *and abound*, they keep you from being ineffective or unfruitful in the knowledge of our Lord Jesus Christ.... Therefore, brethren, be the more zealous to *confirm your call and election*, for *if you do this, you will never fall*; so there will be richly provided for you *an entrance into the eternal kingdom* of our Lord and Savior Jesus Christ" (2 Pet. 1:3, 5–8, 10–11).

We see the Mystery of our cooperation with God's grace in Jesus's parable of the talents as well: A man went on a journey and entrusted differing sums of money to three of his servants. The first servant, receiving five talents (about five thousand dollars), invested them and made five more. The second servant did likewise with the two talents he was given. The third servant, however, buried the one talent he had been entrusted with for fear of losing it. When the man returned to settle accounts he was enraged with the third servant: "[Y]ou ought to have invested my money with the bankers, and at my coming I should have received what was my own with interest. [I'll take the talent from you] and give it to him who has the ten talents. For to every one who has will more be given; but from him who has not, even what he has will be taken away" (Matt 25:27–29).

Father's love for His children.[26] All is grace—even our prayer[27]; and by grace we live in a way that pleases our Father. And the Father, looking at us with eyes full of mercy and love, regards these actions (or works, or deeds) as truly ours.[28]

Jesus was very specific about the criteria by which he will judge us on the Last Day. He will welcome the just with a word of thanks for their untold kindnesses to him—kindnesses he received through his connection to all of humanity. He went on to describe how he will tell the wicked, those condemned to "the eternal fire prepared for the devil and his angels," to leave his sight—they had neglected and rejected him (Matt. 25:41). When they ask, "Lord, when did we see you hungry or thirsty or a stranger or naked or sick or in prison and did not minister to you?" (Matt. 25:44), Jesus will answer, "[A]s you did it not to one of the least of these, you did it not to me" (Matt. 25:45). Our verbal confessions of faith, by themselves, are inadequate. Jesus wants our confession made in our flesh and bone, living as he lived; to do otherwise is to reject him. The author of Hebrews took this for granted, encouraging the recipients of his letter: "God is not so unjust as to overlook your work and the love which you showed for his sake in serving the saints, as you still do. And we

26. Scott Hahn, *Hail Holy Queen: The Mother of God in the Word of God* (San Francisco: Doubleday, 2001), 133–4.

27. "God has sent the Spirit of his Son into our hearts, crying, 'Abba! Father!'" (Gal. 4:6).

"[T]he Spirit helps us in our weakness; for we do not know how to pray as we ought, but the Spirit himself intercedes for us with sighs too deep for words. And he who searches the hearts of men knows what is the mind of the Spirit, for the Spirit intercedes for the saints according to the will of God" (Rom. 8:26–27).

28. How can an action be simultaneously God's and ours? Allow me to offer an analogy: Suppose you and your sister were standing at the top of a flight of steps when she lost her balance and began to fall. You reached out and grabbed her, pulling her back upright. In her gratefulness she planted a big kiss on your hand, saying, "I love this hand. Thank you for grabbing me." The good deed took place because of the instrumentality of your hand; it extended toward her and grabbed onto her. But the only way it could perform the good deed was because it participated in your life and was under your direction. The action simultaneously belonged completely to you and completely to your hand. It is akin to the mystery of biblical inspiration: The biblical authors functioned as true human authors, although God is recognized as the *primary* author of their texts.

desire each one of you to show the same earnestness in realizing the full assurance of hope until the end, so that you may not be sluggish, but imitators of those who through faith and patience inherit the promises" (Heb. 6:10–12).

This is why the Epistle of James taught "that a man is justified by works and *not by faith alone.* . . . For as the body apart from the spirit is dead, so faith apart from works is dead" (James 2:24, 26). James was not teaching that we can earn *initial* justification (the gifts of faith and baptism); no, we have been made God's children purely by His favor. What he taught, and the Catholic Church has continually borne witness to, is that justification is not only our unmerited incorporation into Jesus's Sonship; justification *is also* the process of his life fully becoming ours. Jesus did not pour himself out to the Father just interiorly, spiritually, one time at the beginning of his life. He gave himself in his flesh and blood, his words, thoughts and actions continually; and as members of his Body, motivated and empowered by his grace, we are called to do the same![29]

The life of Abraham illustrates the progressive nature of justification. The Epistle to the Hebrews tells us that Abraham first exercised his faith when God called him, at age seventy-five, to leave Haran and set out for a new land that the Lord would show him (Heb. 11:8; Gen. 12:1–4). That was Abraham's initial justification. St. Paul, in his Epistle to the Romans, tells us that Abraham was further justified when, some years later, he put his faith in God's promise to make him the father of a multitude: "Abraham believed God and it was reckoned to him as righteousness" (Rom. 4:3; Gen. 15:6).[30] St. James, in his epistle, tells us that Abraham was justified *yet again* decades later because of his obedience to God's command:

> Was not Abraham our father justified by works, when he offered his son Isaac upon the altar? You see that faith was active along with his works, and faith was completed by works, and Scripture

29. Galatians 5:5–6, "For through the Spirit, by faith, we wait for the *hope* of *righteousness*. For in Christ Jesus neither circumcision nor uncircumcision is of any avail, but *faith working through love.*"

30. Paul further stressed that Abraham's justification occurred completely apart from observance of the Torah (which was not given for another four centuries).

was fulfilled which says, "Abraham believed God and it was reckoned to him as righteousness" and he was called the friend of God. You see that a man is justified by works and not by faith alone. (James 2:21–24)

Such a progression is also seen in the life of St. Paul. He wrote to the Philippians, "Not that I have already obtained this or am already perfect; but I press on to make it my own, because Christ Jesus has made me his own. . . . I press on toward the goal for the prize of the upward call of God in Christ Jesus" (Phil. 3:12, 14). Years later, though, Paul was able to tell Timothy, "I am already on the point of being sacrificed. . . . I have fought the good fight, I have finished the race, I have kept the faith. From now on there is laid up for me the crown of righteousness, which the Lord, the righteous judge, will award me on that Day" (2 Tim. 4:6–8). Paul had fully entered into Jesus's offering to the Father. If we enter into Jesus's offering by obedience to God's will and persevere through suffering, then we too will share his Resurrection (Phil. 2:8–9; 3:10–11).

We must never take our salvation for granted, because justification can be lost. We have already read many warnings to this effect from the author of Hebrews (2:1–3, 3:6–14, 4:11, 6:4–12); and we do so in this portion of the epistle as well:

A man who violated the law of Moses dies without mercy at the testimony of two or three witnesses. How much worse punishment do you think will be deserved by the man who has spurned the Son of God, and profaned the blood of the covenant by which he was sanctified, and outraged the Spirit of grace? . . . Therefore do not throw away your confidence, which has a great reward. For you have need of endurance, so that you may do the will of God and receive what is promised. [The prophet Habakkuk wrote,] "For yet a little while, and the coming one shall come and shall not tarry; but my righteous one shall live by faith, and if he shrinks back, my soul has no pleasure in him."[31] But we are not of those who shrink back and are destroyed, but of those who have faith and keep their souls. (Heb. 10:28–29, 35–39)

31. You now understand why Paul's quotation of Habakkuk, "the righteous shall live by faith," in Romans 1:17 and Galatians 3:11 cannot be construed as teaching that final justification is a matter of faith *alone*.

The author of Hebrews wants us to have tremendous confidence in Christ's power to save us, but to also be cognizant of the danger of abandoning Christ through apostasy or the commission of a deadly sin (1 John 5:16). St. Paul produced lists of such mortal sins.[32] Such sins, if freely engaged in, with prior knowledge of their seriousness, strangle the supernatural life within us. If we die prior to repenting of them, then we will suffer eternal separation from God, hell.[33] Let us not forget that there is a devil who tempted our first parents to sin, and that he and his cohorts are actively working to bring us to ruin (Heb. 2:14–15; 1 Pet. 5:8).

Part of the gospel message is that we do not struggle against threats, temptations, and the demonic alone, but as members of Christ's mystical Body, the new and living Temple (Eph. 1:22–23, 2:21–22). Above we read Jesus's words at the Last Supper: "As the branch cannot bear fruit by itself, unless it abides in the vine, neither can you, unless you *abide* in me" (John 15:4). In John's Gospel,

---

32. "Do you not know that the unrighteous will not inherit the kingdom of God? Do not be deceived; neither the immoral, nor idolaters, nor adulterers, nor [practicing] homosexuals, nor thieves, nor greedy, nor drunkards, nor revilers, nor robbers will inherit the kingdom of God" (1 Cor. 6:9–10).

"Now the works of the flesh are plain: immorality, impurity, licentiousness, idolatry, sorcery, enmity, strife, jealousy, anger, selfishness, dissension, party spirit, envy, drunkenness, carousing, and the like. I warn you, as I warned you before, that those who do such things shall not inherit the kingdom of God" (Gal. 5:19–21).

33. Scripture illustrates this fact. One verse some have appealed to in attempting to show that salvation cannot be forfeited is 1 John 5:13: "I write this to you who believe in the name of the Son of God, that you may know that you *have* eternal life." I agree wholeheartedly; anyone in relationship with Christ possesses life himself. But notice that John did not say that rejecting the Lord was impossible. In fact, the same epistle contains a number of verses where he clearly states that our relationship to the Father is conditional upon our maintaining a lifestyle consistent with the Gospel; see 1 John 1:7; 2:5–6; 2:24.

Consider the warnings Jesus gave in the gospels: "Because wickedness is multiplied, most men's love will grow cold. But he who *endures to the end* will be saved" (Matt. 24:12–13); "watch at all times, praying that you may have the strength to escape all these things that will take place, and stand before the Son of man" (Lk. 21:36).

The apostles of course agreed with Jesus. St. James wrote, "[D]esire when it is conceived gives birth to sin, and sin when it is full-grown brings forth death" (James 1:15). Paul was quite blunt: "I pommel my body and subdue it, *lest after*

the word "abide" appears in only one place outside the Last Supper—in Jesus's Bread of Life Discourse: "[M]y flesh is food indeed, and my blood is drink indeed. He who eats my flesh and drinks my blood abides in me, and I in him. As the living Father sent me, and I live because of the Father, so he who eats me will live because of me" (John 6:55–57).[34] Salvation is not meant to occur in isolation. Coming together as a Church to celebrate the Eucharist and enter into Christ's sacrifice on the Lord's Day, to hear God's Word proclaimed, to pray for and encourage one another—these are the normal means of growing in grace and avoiding a fall. As members of Christ's body, cells of his mystical humanity, we act as conduits of God's grace to one another:

> [Jesus] gave some as apostles, others as prophets, others as evange-
> lists, others as pastors and teachers, *to equip the holy ones for the*

---

preaching to others I myself should be disqualified" (1 Cor. 9:27); "[A]ll passed through the sea, and all were baptized into Moses in the cloud and in the sea, and all ate the same supernatural food. . . . Nevertheless with most of them God was not pleased; for 'they were overthrown in the wilderness.' Now these things are a warning *for us*. . . . they were written down for our instruction, upon whom the end of the ages has come. Therefore, *let any one who thinks that he stands take heed lest he fall*" (1 Cor. 10:1–3, 5–6, 11–12). Peter was equally plain: "For if, after they have escaped the defilements of the world through the knowledge of our Lord and Savior Jesus Christ, they are *again entangled* in them and overpowered, the last state has become worse for them than the first. For it would have been better for them never to have known the way of righteousness than after knowing it *to turn back from the holy commandment delivered to them*" (2 Pet. 2:20–21); "beware lest you be carried away with the error of lawless men and *lose your own stability*" (2 Pet. 3:17–18).

Some groups of non-Catholic Christians try to side-step these verses by claiming that the guilty must never have been authentic Christians. On the contrary, the Lord Jesus addressed his warnings to his apostles and disciples, and the apostles wrote their epistles to committed members of the Church. When men and women become Christians they retain their free wills. And *because they have free will*, they continue to have the ability to reject God's offer of eternal life. Consider Genesis' story of the fall. Our first parents were molded and fashioned by God and filled with sanctifying grace. They lived in intimate union with God and one another; and yet, they yielded to temptation—cutting themselves off from the life of God and bringing spiritual death to our race. If they could be in the state of grace and subsequently fall, then the same is true of us.

34. My thanks to Marcus Grodi for this insight.

work of ministry, for building up the body of Christ, until we all attain to the unity of faith and knowledge of the Son of God, to mature manhood, to the extent of the full stature of Christ… from whom the whole body, joined and held together by every supporting ligament, *with the proper functioning of each part, brings about the body's growth and builds itself up in love.* (Eph. 4:11–13, 16)[35]

When we face grave illness, the presbyters of the Church are there to communicate God's strength in the anointing of the sick (James 5:13–16).[36] And if we succumb to mortal sin, then the sacrament of reconciliation is available to heal us (John 20:22–23).

Again, this entire process that I have described was encapsulated by the author of Hebrews:

HEBREWS 10:19–23	SALVATION UNDER THE NEW COVENANT
Therefore, brethren, since we have confidence to enter the [heavenly] sanctuary by the blood of Jesus, by the new and living way which he opened for us through the curtain, that is, through his flesh, and since we have a great high priest over the house of God, let us draw near with a true heart in full assurance of faith, with our hearts sprinkled clean from an evil conscience and our bodies washed with pure water. Let us hold fast the confession of our hope without wavering, for he who promised is faithful; and let us consider how to stir up one another to love and good works, not neglecting to meet together, as is the habit of some, but encouraging one another, and all the more as you see the Day drawing near.	Jesus's life, offered to the Father in the power of the Holy Spirit, merited salvation for the human race. We are united to Christ and first receive salvation through the gifts of faith and baptism. His life grows in us through grace-filled works, active membership in his Body, and participation in the Church's Eucharist and sacramental life … until we are united with him in heaven and then share his bodily resurrection on the Last Day.

35. *New American Bible*, revised edition. We, the members of Christ's Church, are even his instruments in bringing others to salvation. See, for example, 1 Cor. 7:16; 1 Tim. 4:16; Jude 22–23.

36. United to Jesus, even our suffering can be of benefit to other members of the

This is the reality to which the Temple, the Torah, and all the prophets pointed (Matt. 13:17). This is the salvation Christ died, rose, and ascended to bring us; and we must never allow ourselves to grow so accustomed to the idea of it that we cease to be in awe. No worldly pleasure or earthly pain should turn us aside from our goal. And by God's grace, it will not:

> Since then we have a great high priest who has passed through the heavens, Jesus, the Son of God, let us hold fast our confession. For we have not a high priest who is unable to sympathize with our weaknesses, but one who in every respect has been tempted as we are, yet without sinning. Let us then with confidence draw near to the throne of grace, that we may receive mercy and find grace to help in time of need. (Heb. 4:14–16)

Body: "Now I rejoice in my sufferings for your sake, and in my flesh I complete what is lacking in Christ's afflictions for the sake of his body, that is, the Church" (Col. 1:24). One can find further information on this aspect of our union with Christ in my *Through, With, and In Him* (Kettering, OH: Angelico Press, 2014), 109–110.

5

The Communion of Saints

HEBREWS, CHAPTERS 11–12

Therefore, since we are surrounded by so great a cloud of witnesses, let us also lay aside every weight, and sin which clings so closely, and let us run with perseverance the race that is set before us.

⁓*Hebrews* 12:1

✢

We now turn our attention to the way the author of Hebrews encouraged and challenged his readers by reminding them of Israel's great champions of faith. Seemingly insurmountable obstacles were par for the course under the Old Covenant, and they would be so under the New as well. Trials, rather than stifle the great people of the past, called them to exercise their faith and, by doing so, reach spiritual maturity. Christ has united us to them in one great family; and they now cheer us on from heaven, the true Holy of Holies to which Christ has given them access. The Catholic Church calls this reality the communion of saints. With the author of Hebrews as guide we will come to a deeper understanding of this communion and the benefits it affords us. We will also look at the purification that, if needed, the Lord will make available to us at the end of our lives so that we too will be capable of experiencing heavenly life.

Past Champions of Faith

The eleventh chapter of Hebrews is focused upon the faith of the ancients. It is the continuation of a passage we looked at in our discussion of justification:

> [D]o not throw away your confidence, which has a great reward. For you have need of endurance, so that you may do the will of

God and receive what is promised. [The prophet Habakkuk wrote,] "For yet a little while, and the coming one shall come and shall not tarry; but my righteous one shall live by faith, and if he shrinks back, my soul has no pleasure in him." But we are not of those who shrink back and are destroyed, but of those who have faith and keep their souls. (Heb. 10:35–39)

Our author immediately continues:

Now faith is *the assurance of things hoped for, the conviction of things not seen*. For by it the men of old received divine approval. (Heb. 11:1–2)

That was the type of faith his readers needed to possess if they were to weather persecution and obtain their heavenly inheritance. Before the eyes of the world—the Jewish and Roman authorities—Jesus had been crucified as a criminal, his message discredited, and his fledgling movement was on the verge of being stamped out. In stark contrast, *through the eyes of faith*, the early Church saw Jesus resurrected, seated upon his heavenly throne, and ready to vindicate his faithful.[1] God's children had to walk by faith, not sight (2 Cor. 5:7), because *reality* was far different than what they would conclude from earthly experience.

The author reminds his readers that it had always been this way. He leads them through a list of Israel's heroes, introducing each with the phrase, "By faith…" and then recounting his or her mighty deeds. Since you can refer to the chapter, I will not recount every example; but I do wish to draw your attention to at least a few. They highlight how our faith in God's revelation demands action.

Let us start with the heroes written of in the Torah. Our first figure should be familiar to all:

By faith Noah, being warned by God concerning events *as yet unseen*, took heed and constructed an ark for the saving of his household; by this he condemned the world and became an heir of the righteousness which comes by faith. (11:7)

1. The early Church understood the Roman destruction of Jerusalem as Jesus coming in judgment upon the unrepentant city and its leaders; see Matthew 24:15–34.

He then appealed to the faith of the patriarchs:

> By faith Abraham obeyed when he was called to go out to a place which he was to receive as an inheritance; and he went out, not knowing where he was to go. By faith he sojourned in the land of promise, as in a foreign land, living in tents with Isaac and Jacob, heirs with him of the same promise. *For he looked forward to the city* which has foundations, *whose builder and maker is God.* (11:8–10)

> By faith [his wife] Sarah herself received power to conceive, even when she was past the age, since *she considered him faithful who had promised.* (11:11)

He reminds his readers—some of whom had been dispossessed of their land (10:34)—how:

> These all died in faith, not having received what was promised, but having seen it and greeted it from afar, and having acknowledged that they were *strangers and exiles on the earth.* For people who speak thus make it clear that they are seeking a homeland. If they had been thinking of that land from which they had gone out, they would have had opportunity to return. But as it is, they desire a better country, that is, *a heavenly one.* Therefore God is not ashamed to be called their God, for he has prepared for them *a city.* (11:13–16)

The most astounding show of patriarchal faith was what the Jewish people came to refer to as the *Akedah,* or the *binding* of Isaac:

> By faith Abraham, when he was tested, offered up Isaac, and he who had received the promises was ready to offer up his only-begotten son, of whom it was said, "Through Isaac shall your descendants be named." He considered that God was able to raise men even from the dead; hence he did receive him back and this was a symbol. (11:17–19)

From the patriarchs, our author directs his readers' attention to the faith of Moses:

> By faith Moses, when he was grown up, refused to be called the son of Pharaoh's daughter, choosing rather to share ill-treatment with the people of God than to enjoy the fleeting pleasures of sin.

85

He considered abuse suffered for the Christ greater wealth than the treasures of Egypt, for he looked to the reward. By faith he left Egypt, not being afraid of the anger of the king; for he endured as *seeing him who is invisible.* (11:24–27)

Our author then offers, in quick succession, a litany of great saints and the mighty deeds faith allowed them to accomplish. All possessed what the Christian of today would call a "saving" faith. We saw in the last chapter how Scripture affirmed such faith of Abraham, and we find it affirmed here of Noah ("the righteousness that comes by faith") and numerous others. In fact, their faith in God's heretofore partial revelation was an implicit faith *in the Christ* who would complete Revelation. Despite that implicit faith, God, in his wisdom, postponed their entrance into the "city," the heavenly homeland. "All these, though well attested by their faith, *did not receive what was promised*, since God had foreseen something better for us, that *apart from us* they should not be made perfect" (11:39–40).

From Sheol *to the Heavenly Jerusalem*

Unlike most ancient peoples, the early Israelites had little to say regarding the afterlife. In the earliest strata of the OT we hear of *Sheol* (translated *Hades* in the Septuagint), the abode of the dead.[2] It was a gloomy realm where, separated from their bodies, the dead were shadows of their former selves (Is. 14:9–11). Those who "descended" to *Sheol*, both the just and the wicked, were at a distance from God (Ps. 6:5; Ps. 88:5, 10–12).[3] Not until the Babylonian

---

2. *Sheol* is the most common OT term for the realm of the dead, but one also finds the synonyms *Bôr* (Pit), *Sahat* (Pit), and *Abbadon* (Destruction). For a breakdown of OT references to *Sheol* according to their various emphasis and synonyms, see Philip S. Johnston, *Shades of Sheol: Death and Afterlife in the Old Testament* (Downers Grove, IL: InterVarsity Press, 2002), 80–85.

3. The great exceptions to this were the OT figures who were assumed, body and soul, into heaven: Enoch (Gen. 5:24; Sir. 44:16; Sir. 49:14; Heb. 11:5) and Elijah (2 Kings 2:11; 1 Macc. 2:58). Moses may have been a third person raised into heaven, but only after first experiencing death. The Babylonian Talmud recorded the tradition that Moses was assumed, and there is an intriguing passage in Jude 9, as well as Moses's appearance along with Elijah (whom we know to have been assumed) at Jesus's transfiguration, which may point in that direction.

exile do we find the revelation that God would one day raise the dead and pronounce judgment upon them. In Daniel we read:

[A]t that time your people shall be delivered, every one whose name shall be found written in the book. And many of those who sleep in the dust of the earth shall awake, some to everlasting life, and some to shame and everlasting contempt. (Dan. 12:1-2)

By the time the Wisdom of Solomon was composed (ca. 100 BC), we have written evidence that, at least among some groups of Jews, there was a growing realization that the lots of the righteous and of the wicked in *Sheol* prior to the resurrection and judgment were not identical. The just, although not admitted into God's heavenly presence, still experienced His care:

[T]he souls of the righteous are in the hand of God, / and no torment will ever touch them. / In the eyes of the foolish they seemed to have died, / and their departure was thought to be an affliction, / and their going out from us to be their destruction; / *but they are at peace* /. . . . In the time of their visitation [at the resurrection], they will shine forth, / and will run like sparks through the stubble. / They will govern nations and rule over peoples, / and the Lord will reign over them for ever. (Wis. 3:1–3, 7–8)

God's faithful ones were at peace, but not inactive. Second Maccabees, composed at approximately the same time as Wisdom, tells how the revered freedom fighter, Judas Maccabeus,

. . . cheered [his soldiers] by relating a dream, a sort of vision, which was worthy of belief. What he saw was this: Onias, [the deceased] high priest, a noble and good man . . . was praying with outstretched hands for the whole body of the Jews. Then likewise a man appeared, distinguished by his grey hair and dignity, and of marvelous majesty and authority. And Onias spoke, saying, "This is a man who loves the brethren and prays much for the people and the holy city, Jeremiah, the prophet of God." (2 Macc. 15:11–14)

Over the next hundred years the Jewish understanding of *Sheol* continued to be refined. The first portion of the popular *Book of Enoch* (quoted in the NT's Epistle of Jude) showed the souls of the dead separated into four different caverns, one for the righteous and three for different classes of sinners.[4] In Jesus's parable of the rich man and Lazarus, the good and wicked in *Hades* are separated by a "great chasm" (Lk. 16:26). The deceased Lazarus is "comforted" in "Abraham's bosom," while the rich man is in "anguish," in "flames" (Lk. 16:24–25). Likewise, when Jesus was on the Cross, he promised the repentant thief, "[T]oday you will be with me in Paradise" (Lk. 23:43).[5]

When Jesus died, his soul did not enter into heavenly glory, but descended to *Sheol*.[6] We read how, at Jesus's death on Good Friday, the veil before the Holy of Holies was rent in two, indicating that humanity's sin had been atoned for and humanity's path to the heavenly Father opened. Jesus went in search of the souls of his beloved friends, the just who had awaited his coming. This is what the Apostle's Creed means when it says Christ "descended into hell." I would be hard-pressed to explain Jesus's sojourn more clearly than the *Catechism of the Catholic Church*—note its application of the Epistle to the Hebrews:

> This is the last phase of Jesus' messianic mission, a phase that is condensed in time but vast in its real significance: the spread of Christ's redemptive work to all men of all times and places, for all who are saved have been made sharers in redemption. Christ went down into the depths of death so that "the dead will hear the voice

4. George Foot Moore, *Judaism in the First Centuries of the Christian Era*, vol. 2 (New York: Schocken Books, 1971), 302.

5. Also, in Jesus's prayer from the Cross, "Father, into your hands I commit my spirit" (Lk. 23:46), we hear not just a quotation of Psalm 31:5, but an echo of Wisdom 3:1, quoted above, which states that even in *Sheol*, the souls of the righteous were "in the hand of God."

6. See 1 Pet. 3:18–19; 1 Pet. 4:6; Eph. 4:9; and Luke 16:22. The Scriptural data is neatly summarized in CCC 633: "Scripture calls the abode of the dead, to which the dead Christ went down, 'hell'—Sheol in Hebrew or Hades in Greek—because those who are there are deprived of the vision of God. Such is the case for all the dead, whether evil or righteous, while they await the Redeemer: which does not mean that their lot is identical, as Jesus shows through the parable of the poor man Lazarus who was received into 'Abraham's bosom': 'It is precisely these holy souls, who awaited their Savior in Abraham's bosom, whom Christ the Lord delivered when he descended into hell' [*Roman Catechism* I, 6, 3]. Jesus did not descend into hell to deliver the damned, nor to destroy the hell of damnation, but to free the just who had gone before him."

of the Son of God, and those we hear will live" [John 5:25]. Jesus, "the Author of life," by dying destroyed "him who has the power of death, that is, the devil, and [delivered] all those who through fear of death were subject to lifelong bondage" [Heb. 2:14–15]. Henceforth, the risen Christ holds "the keys of Death and Hades." [Rev. 1:18] (CCC 634–35)

All of the heroes of faith to whom the Jewish people looked found their completion in Christ. Jesus ushered them out of *Sheol* and into the land, the city, they had been promised—the *heavenly* Jerusalem. It was the same city to which God called the recipients of the Epistle to the Hebrews, and to which he calls us. As members of Jesus's Body—the Jesus who triumphantly ascended into heaven—we are already mystically present there (Eph. 2:6).

Participants in Jesus's Heavenly Intercession

When you and I pray, when we spiritually draw near God's heavenly throne, we find ourselves surrounded by all those Jesus has led into glory. The author of Hebrews wanted his readers to understand the magnitude of the new order established by Christ—for the faithful of the past and present:

> [Y]ou have come to Mount Zion and to the city of the living God, the heavenly Jerusalem, and to innumerable angels in festal gathering . . . and to the spirits of *just men made perfect*, and to Jesus the mediator of a new covenant. (Heb. 12:22–23)

St. Paul alluded to this same truth when he wrote how, when he prayed, he knelt "before the Father, from whom his whole family in heaven and on earth derives its name" (Eph. 3:14).[7] We see something of it in the gospels as well: when Jesus prayed to the Father on the mount of transfiguration, Moses and Elijah participated in their conversation (Lk. 9:29–31).

The imagery used by the author of Hebrews corresponds perfectly with what we find in the Book of Revelation. It too is concerned with the heavenly Jerusalem (Rev. 3:12, 21:2). When Jesus

---

7. New International Version.

summoned John to heaven, John saw the reality upon which the Tabernacle and Temple had been patterned. There, in the true Holy of Holies, John beheld not only the "sea" (Rev. 4:6), the seven-branched lampstand (4:5), the altar of incense (8:3–4), trumpets, golden bowls, and angels singing liturgical hymns (4:8,11; 5:9–14; 8:2); but the ascended and glorified Christ, the Lamb of God, pre-senting himself to the Father, his wounds visible (5:6). In short, John saw the eternal liturgy in which Christ Jesus acts as high priest; and there with Jesus, participating in the liturgy, were the men and women he had saved:

> Round [God's] throne were twenty-four thrones, and seated on the thrones were twenty-four elders, clothed in white garments, with golden crowns upon their heads.... [T]he twenty-four elders fall down before him who is seated on the throne and worship him who lives for ever and ever; they cast their crowns before the throne, singing.... (Rev. 4:4, 10)

The number twenty-four represents the founders of Israel's Twelve Tribes joined with Christ's Twelve Apostles—the entire Old Testa-ment and New Testament people of God.[8] Their white garments are those of priests. They throw down their crowns, making a return to the Father of the life and graces he gave them. In doing so they show themselves redeemed from humanity's Fall—its refusal to live in the image of the Son. They offer themselves to the Father in union with Jesus. They share his priesthood, the priesthood of Melchizedek— based not upon Levitical descent, but the "indestructible life" of Christ (Heb. 7:16), imparted to them in baptism.

Since Christ "lives to make intercession for" us (Heb. 7:25), it only makes sense that those who share his life in heaven do the same. And that was what John saw:

> [T]he twenty-four elders fell down before the Lamb. Each one had a harp and they were holding golden bowls full of incense, which are the prayers of God's people. (Rev. 5:8)[9]

---

8. This also corresponded to the twenty-four divisions of priests who served in the Jerusalem Temple (1 Chron. 24:1–31).

9. New International Version.

They fall down before the Lamb, and *through Christ*, our common high priest, present our petitions to Father. This would not have seemed strange to Jewish Christians such as John, since, as we saw above, while in *Sheol* the just had interceded for the living (2 Macc. 15:11–14). It only made sense that, once admitted into God's presence, they would have continued doing so. There, fully united to the Trinity, they love us more, not less. The angels, whom God has charged with our care (Matt. 18:10), also present our prayers:

> Another angel, who had a golden censer, came and stood at the altar. He was given much incense to offer, with the prayers of all God's people, on the golden altar in front of the throne. The smoke of the incense, together with the prayers of God's people, went up before God from the angel's hand. (Rev. 8:3–4)[10]

Christ is our high priest; and *through, with*, and *in him*, the saints and angels in heaven offer our prayers to the Father. We saw earlier how the Greek term *teleiō* ("perfected") was used by the Septuagint in reference to the ordination of priests. With that connotation in mind we have an even greater appreciation of Hebrews' statement that the heavenly Jerusalem is filled with the "the spirits of just men *made perfect*" (Heb. 12:23).

In Christ, we and the saints in heaven form but one mystical Body. This is what the Apostle's Creed and the Catholic Church mean when they speak of the communion of saints. Just as you and I ask our siblings on earth to pray for us, we can ask our siblings in heaven to do the same. Christ connects us to them and appraises them of our struggles (Rev. 6:9–11). The veneration we have for the saints in heaven—those whose faith was expounded upon by the author of Hebrews, as well as all those who have come since—and the intercession they make for us is predicated upon our union in Christ:

> For just as the body is one and has many members, and all the members of the body, though many, are one body, so it is with

---

10. New International Version. Recall that the Levitical priests performed these same actions in the earthly Temple.

Christ . . . there [should] be no discord in the body . . . the members [should] have the same care for one another. If one member suffers, all suffer together; if one member is honored, all rejoice together. (1 Cor. 12:12, 25–26)

The love we on earth have for the saints in heaven (and they for us) is a manifestation of, a participation in, Christ's love for each of us. We fill our churches with their images for the same reason we fill our homes with pictures of our families. When we recount the lives of the saints—as the author of Hebrews did—we celebrate and magnify what *God did* in them.

There is of course no competition between Christ's priestly intercession and that of *his Body*. The prayers of Christ's people, whether they are on earth or in heaven, are a participation in, a manifestation of, his priesthood: "for through him we both have access in one Spirit to the Father" (Eph. 2:18). Paul told his young bishop, Timothy,

First of all, then, I urge that supplications, prayers, intercessions, and thanksgivings be made for all men, for kings and all who are in high positions. . . . This is good, and it is acceptable in the sight of God our Savior, who desires all men to be saved and to come to the knowledge of the truth. For there is one God, and there is *one mediator between God and men, the man Christ Jesus.* . . . I desire then that in every place the men should pray, lifting holy hands without anger or quarreling. . . . (1 Tim. 2:1–5, 8)

Because Christ is our mediator with the Father, *because he lives within us*, we can pray and petition God to pour out the grace of salvation upon others. It is Christ's eternal intercession, manifested in the members of his Body.

Jesus inaugurated a completely new phase in salvation history. United to him, both we and the saints of the past have access to the Father's throne in heaven, the fulfillment of the Temple's Holy of Holies and the homeland promised to Abraham and his descendants. As it did for our ancestors, our faith should embolden us to continue professing and living our religion despite external opposition, and to conquer sin and vice within ourselves:

Therefore, since we are surrounded by so great a cloud of witnesses,[11] let us also lay aside every weight, and sin which clings so closely, and let us run with perseverance the race that is set before us, looking to Jesus the pioneer and perfecter of our faith, who for the joy that was set before him endured the cross, despising the shame, and is seated at the right hand of the throne of God. Consider him who endured from sinners such hostility against himself, so that you may not grow weary or fainthearted. (Heb. 12:1–3)

The Purgative Way

The incredible trials faced by the early Church—the difficulties faced by us today—are meant to detach us from sin and force us to grow strong in the grace of Christ. Outright persecution quickly divests us of the illusion that compromise with the values of a fallen world is possible (1 John 2:15–17; 4:4–6). God does not set these trials in motion; but in his providence he harnesses them to burn away the dross in our souls:

> It is for discipline that you have to endure. God is treating you as sons; for what son is there whom his father does not discipline?... [W]e have had earthly fathers to discipline us and we respected them. Shall we not much more be subject to the Father of spirits and live? For they disciplined us for a short time at their pleasure, but he disciplines us for our good, that we may *share his holiness.* (Heb. 12:7, 9–10)

Holiness is about more than simply eliminating sin from our lives. That is its necessary first element; but if holiness consisted solely in giving up negative behaviors, we would do nothing more than create a void. Jesus warned against this:

> When the unclean spirit has gone out of a man, he passes through waterless places seeking rest, but he finds none. Then he says, "I will return to my house from which I came." And when he comes he finds it empty, swept and put in order. Then he goes and brings with him seven other spirits more evil than himself, and they enter and dwell there; and the last state of that man becomes worse than the first.... (Matt. 12:43–45)

11. The saints of the past have entered, with Jesus, into the "cloud" of God's glory (Ex. 14:20; 1 Kings 8:10; Luke 9:34–35; Acts 1:9).

Holiness is, most importantly, about that with which we are filled. As we said in chapter four, the Holy Spirit constantly prompts us to display Christ's life and character; and we are meant to cooperate with Him in the hard work of growing in virtue. It is one thing to do so when conditions are fair; but judging from the lives of the saints, God knows there is nothing as effective for *cementing* virtue in the soul as trials and difficulties. They are the "resistance training" of the spiritual life:

> "My child, when you come to serve the Lord, prepare yourself for trials /. . . . Cling to him, do not leave him, that you may prosper in your last days. / Accept whatever happens to you; in periods of humiliation be patient. / For in fire gold is tested, and the chosen, in the crucible of humiliation. / Trust in God, and he will help you." (Sir. 2:1, 3–6)[12]

St. Peter echoes this imagery of gold tested in fire, going on to say that trials should fill us with joy as we anticipate the heavenly life with which our faithfulness will be rewarded (1 Pet. 1:6–7).

Earthly difficulties compel us to grapple with profound spiritual truths. They force us to recognize our frailty. True strength does not come from us, and we cannot count upon the weak resources of a fallen world. God, and God alone, is the source of the Church's life (Ps. 20:7; Isa. 31:1). It is impossible for this world, as it presently exists, to satisfy us. Our souls are longing for a salvation that can only be realized outside of history, when Jesus brings the heavenly Jerusalem to earth.[13] Times of trouble should cause us to draw even closer to God through prayer, the sacraments, and meditation upon his Word. Saint Paul candidly recounts his personal experience of trial and its benefits:

> [T]o keep me from being too elated by the abundance of revelations, a thorn was given me in the flesh, a messenger of Satan, to harass me, to keep me from being too elated. Three times I begged the Lord about this, that it should leave me; but he said to me, "My grace is sufficient for you, for my power is made perfect in weak-

---

12. New American Bible, revised edition.
13. Hebrews 11:10, 13:14; Rev. 21:1–2; CCC 676–7.

ness." I will all the more gladly boast of my weaknesses, that the power of Christ may rest upon me. For the sake of Christ, then, I am content with weaknesses, insults, hardships, persecutions, and calamities; for when I am weak, then I am strong. (2 Cor. 12:7–10)

When we suffer, when we endure the Cross in union with Jesus, we take on his image in the most profound way possible. When our petitions for deliverance seem to be met with the same silence as Jesus's in Gethsemane and yet we obediently continue with faith in the Father's love for us, then we are truly conformed to the Master. When we show "love, joy, peace, patience, kindness, goodness, faithfulness, gentleness, [and] self-control"[14] in the midst of suffering, our life's goal is being realized. We are being perfected. Catholics refer to it as the mystery of "redemptive suffering." And somehow, connected as we are in the communion of saints, the graces God gives us in those moments are of benefit to all. Paul wrote, "Now I rejoice in my sufferings for your sake, and in my flesh I complete what is lacking in Christ's afflictions for the sake of his body, that is, the church" (Col. 1:24).

The writer of Hebrews identified his reader's difficulties as God's fatherly discipline (Heb. 12:7–10). He asks us to have faith that, like the great saints of the past, whatever trials God allows us to undergo are meant to yield positive, eternal benefits:

For the moment all discipline seems painful rather than pleasant; later it yields the peaceful fruit of righteousness to those who have been trained by it. Therefore lift your drooping hands and strengthen your weak knees, and make straight paths for your feet, so that what is lame may not be put out of joint but rather be healed. (Heb. 12:11–13)

Note those last words. God *is* going to propel us forward—whether we like it and feel prepared for it, or not. We are meant to "share *his* holiness" (Heb. 12:10), that "holiness *without which* no one will see the Lord" (Heb. 12:14). "[N]othing unclean shall enter" the heavenly Jerusalem—only those who have come to perfectly share Christ's holiness (Rev. 21:27).

---

14. Galatians 5:22–23.

The Reality of Purgatory

I imagine that, reading those words from the Book of Revelation, the majority—if not all—of us feel far from ready to enter heaven. We recognize how imperfectly we offer ourselves to the Father. We fight his efforts to purify us, seeking relief from trials through varying levels of moral compromise. Instead of placing God and his kingdom absolutely first, we fall prey to an inordinate love of ourselves and of created goods. Jesus taught that "from within, *out of the heart of man*, come evil thoughts, fornication, theft, murder, adultery, coveting, wickedness, deceit, licentiousness, envy, slander, pride, foolishness. All these evil things come from *within*, and they defile a man" (Mk. 7:21–23). You and I may not commit murder, but the unkind thoughts and harsh judgments we harbor toward others (the roots of murder) may still be very much with us; and, according to Jesus, they defile us (Matt. 5:21–26). These imperfections do not completely severe our union with the Lord, but they do inhibit the flow of his life within us. If we died at this moment our souls would be *incapable* of fully participating in the life of heaven; they stand in need of transformation.

All Christians are in agreement that those in heaven are completely free of sin, as well as the impulse to sin. Christian communities stemming from the Reformation rarely speak of this, but such a belief presupposes a post-death purification. The Catholic Church, relying on Apostolic Tradition, is more explicit about the process. Over time it came to be called "purgatory."

When we turn to the *Catechism of the Catholic Church*, we find two points affirmed about this post-death purification. First, purgatory does not offer those who have rejected God a second chance at salvation. Rather, it is a "final purification of the *elect*," those who have died "in God's grace and friendship." Second, our brothers and sisters undergoing this purification are united to us in the communion of saints and benefit from our prayers (CCC 1030–32). The Catechism notes that it is common for the Church to speak of purgatory by appropriating the Scriptural image of a cleansing fire.

Saint Paul provided what may be the classic example. Speaking of those who had labored to build up the Christian community at

Corinth, Paul reminded them how he had laid the original foundation, going on to say:

> [I]f any one builds on the foundation with gold, silver, precious stones, wood, hay, straw—each man's work will become manifest; for the Day [of Judgment] will disclose it, because it will be revealed with fire, and the fire will test what sort of work each one has done. If the work which any man has built on the foundation survives, he will receive a reward. If any man's work is burned up, he will suffer loss, though *he himself will be saved*, but only as through *fire*. (1 Cor. 3:12–15)

Paul speaks about the large-scale purifying fire the Church will experience when Christ returns as judge. Purgatory is nothing more than Paul's teaching pared down to the individual soul and the "particular judgment" it undergoes at death.

Cardinal Joseph Ratzinger (later Pope Benedict XVI) draws together all we have seen thus far to arrive at a tremendous insight:

> Purgatory is not ... some kind of supra-worldly concentration camp where one is forced to undergo punishments in a more or less arbitrary fashion. Rather it is the inwardly necessary process of transformation in which a person becomes capable of Christ, capable of God [i.e., capable of full unity with Christ and God] and thus capable of unity with the whole communion of saints. Simply to look at people with any degree of realism at all is to grasp the necessity of such a process.... What actually saves is the full assent of faith. But in most of us, that basic option is buried under a great deal of wood, hay and straw. Only with difficulty can it peer out from behind the latticework of an egoism we are powerless to pull down with our own hands. Man is the recipient of the divine mercy, yet this does not exonerate him from *the need to be transformed*. Encounter with the Lord *is* this transformation. *It is the fire* that burns away our dross and re-forms us to be vessels of eternal joy.[15]

Purgatory is not separation from Christ, but a transformative encounter with him. This brings us back to the very section of

---

15. Joseph Ratzinger, *Eschatology: Death and Eternal Life* (Washington, DC: The Catholic University of America Press, 2007), 230–1.

Hebrews under consideration and its claim that "*our God* is a consuming fire" (Heb. 12:29). As the impurities within our souls are burned away we will likely experience discomfort; seeing ourselves as we truly are before God's righteous eyes always entails discomfort. What remains after the purification, however, will be hearts finally able to embrace the Lord without the slightest reservation.

None of this would have sounded strange to Jewish ears since the souls in *Sheol*—the souls that Christ admitted to heaven—were already thought to undergo purification. Earlier I noted that by the time of Jesus, some Jews (Jesus among them) held that the just and wicked had vastly different experiences of *Sheol*, with the wicked being in flames (Lk. 16:24–25). In the generation before Christ, the school of Shammai, a revered rabbi, had taught that the souls of those among the chosen people whose actions had been an admixture of good and evil were purified after the manner of gold and silver by being immersed in and then withdrawn from the fires experienced by the wicked.[16] Belief that the dead could be purified from sin actually predated the School of Shammai by at least a century, though. Scripture tells how, after a number of Judas Maccabeus's soldiers fell in battle, he and his men

> turned to prayer begging that the sin which had been committed might be wholly blotted out. . . . [Judas] also took up a collection, man by man, to the amount of two thousand drachmas of silver, and sent it to Jerusalem to provide for a sin offering. In doing this he acted very well and honorably, taking account of the resurrection. . . . Therefore he made atonement for the dead, that they might be delivered from their sin. (2 Macc. 12:42–43, 46)

Those who lived before Christ were ultimately cleansed of their sin in preparation for the resurrection; we now understand that, in anticipation of that Day, their purification allowed them to enter heaven in union with Christ and participate in his kingly and priestly (Melchizedekan) reign.

---

16. George Foot Moore, *Judaism in the First Centuries of the Christian Era*, vol. 2 (New York: Schocken Books, 1971), 318; *Encyclopaedia Judaica*, s.v. "Netherworld" (Jerusalem: Keter Publishing House, 1972).

Like Judas Maccabeus and his men, Christians have always offered prayers on behalf of their deceased brothers and sisters. Saint Paul prayed for God's mercy on the soul of his co-worker Onesiphorus (2 Tim. 1:18), who apparently died between Paul's first and second epistles to Timothy (2 Tim. 1:16, 4:19).[17] We possess ample evidence that the early Church prayed for the dead: the inscription on the burial monument of Abercius, Bishop of Hierapolis (ca. AD 190), *The Acts of Perpetua and Felicity* (ca. 202), as well as the writings of Tertullian (*The Crown*, ca. 211), Cyril of Jerusalem (*Catechetical Discourses*, ca. 350), and Augustine of Hippo (*Care That Should Be Taken of the Dead*, ca. 412). The Church made intercession for the dead, especially during its celebration of the Eucharist on the anniversaries of their deaths.[18]

Mary in the Communion of Saints

It would be negligent to bring a chapter on the communion of saints to an end without at least directing your eyes to its most esteemed member—Mary, the Mother of the Word Incarnate.[19] Although the Epistle to the Hebrews does not mention her by name, its quotation of Psalm 45:6–7 (Heb. 1:8–9) opens the door for us to speak of her.[20] That psalm, which hints at the divinity of the future Davidic King, goes on to speak of his queen mother (the *gebirah*): "at your right hand stands the queen in gold of Ophir" (45:9). As the mother of the successor to David's throne, Mary holds that royal office (1 Kings 2:19; Luke 1:32–33, 43).

Furthermore, her faith in the midst of trial surpassed that of Israel's greatest heroes. Unlike the barren Sarah who laughed when

17. Stephen K. Ray has assembled quotations from a number of notable Protestant and Catholic commentaries that interpret 2 Tim. 1:16–18 in this manner: http://www.catholic-convert.com/wp-content/uploads/Documents/Onesiphorus1.pdf.

18. Kapler, *The God Who is Love*, 115–116.

19. Mary contained the Word within herself—the fulfillment, the embodiment of the Ark of the Covenant (containing the words of the Commandments) of which we have already spoken. Observe how Luke's Gospel (1:35, 39–45, 46) presents her as such via a tapestry of OT illusions and quotations (Exod. 40:34; 2 Sam. 6:2–16).

20. Tim Staples, *Behold Your Mother: A Biblical and Historical Defense of the Marian Doctrines* (El Cajon, CA: Catholic Answers Press, 2014), 280–281.

God promised her a son (Heb. 11:11; Gen. 18:10–14), Mary believed that God could cause even a virgin to conceive (Lk. 1:38, 45). When God asked Abraham to sacrifice his only son, Abraham agreed; but in the end, he was spared the pain of Isaac's death. Mary was not; she saw her Son's sacrifice through to the bitter end. She stood beneath Jesus's cross as he hung there—his body torn, blood flowing down his limbs, suffocating under his own weight. Mary knows the pain of redemptive suffering like no one else. A "sword" pierced her soul so "that thoughts out of many hearts" might be revealed (Lk. 2:35)—yours and mine among them. And like us, Mary accomplished all this not through her own power, but by the *grace of God* (Lk. 1:28)!

The Lord places her before us to show the great heights to which faith can lead the humble. Mary—like Enoch, Elijah, and a number of saints before her (Matt. 27:52–53)—was allowed to share Jesus's bodily triumph over the grave and glorification in heaven. She sits enthroned at his right hand, crowned with glory and honor (Rev. 3:21, 12:1–5). She participates in his priestly intercession for the Church—for its members struggling on earth and those being purified by Christ's fiery love in purgatory (John 2:3–11). They, too, are her children (John 19:25–28; Rev. 12:17).

Let us emulate her faith and invoke her intercession—she from whom Jesus received his body and blood—as we turn our attention to the Eucharist.

6

The Eucharist

We have an altar from which those who serve the tent have no right to eat. ⁓*Hebrews* 13:10

✝

The *Catechism of the Catholic Church* identifies the Eucharist as "the source and summit of the Christian life,"[1] explaining that it contains "*the whole spiritual good of the Church*, namely *Christ himself*, our Pasch" (1324). The Eucharist "is the culmination both of God's action sanctifying the world in Christ and of the worship men offer to Christ and through him to the Father in the Holy Spirit" (1325). In it, "we already unite ourselves with the heavenly liturgy and anticipate eternal life, when God will be all in all" (1326).

If that is truly the case, then why is Hebrews' most overt reference to the Eucharist the verse with which I started the chapter? Recall that our author felt no need to address the "elementary doctrines of Christ" (6:1); and nothing was more elementary, more constitutive, of the early Church than her weekly celebration of the Eucharist (Acts 2:42, 20:7; 1 Cor. 11:23–26). The Epistle to the Hebrews is an extended meditation on the "New Covenant" established by Christ; the only time we find those words on the lips of Jesus himself, however, is when he instituted the Eucharist.[2] The Eucharistic assembly was the presupposition underlying the writing of Hebrews: it was where the epistle would have been read![3] And as we shall see in the

1. The *Catechism* here quotes the Second Vatican Council's *Dogmatic Constitution on the Church*, 11.

2. This is true for all four of the institution narratives that have come down to us: Matt. 26:28; Mark 14:24; Luke 22:20; 1 Cor. 11:25.

3. See Acts 20:27 and 1 Tim. 4:13.

course of this chapter, the Eucharist was integral to the Jewish-Christian understanding of Jesus's execution as a sacrifice, and throws additional light on his designation as a priest in the order of Melchizedek. As the second-century bishop, Irenaeus, wrote, "Our way of thinking is attuned to the Eucharist, and the Eucharist in turn confirms our way of thinking."[4]

Partners in the Altar

I identified Hebrews 13:10 as the epistle's only overt reference to the Eucharist; but we are able to glean more on the subject when we look at the verse in context. I will highlight elements of special interest:

> It is good for our hearts to be strengthened by grace, not by eating ceremonial foods, which is of no benefit to those who do so. *We have an altar* from which those who minister at the tabernacle *have no right to eat.* The high priest carries the blood of animals into the Most Holy Place as a sin offering, but the bodies are burned outside the camp. And so Jesus also suffered outside the city gate to make the people holy through his own blood. Let us, then, go to him outside the camp, bearing the disgrace he bore. For here we do not have an enduring city, but we are looking for the city that is to come. Through Jesus, therefore, let us continually offer to God a *sacrifice of praise*—the fruit of lips that openly profess his name. (Heb. 13:9–15)[5]

We have said that Hebrews was written to strengthen Jewish Christians who, in the face of persecution, were tempted to renounce Christ and return to the synagogue and Temple from which they had been ostracized. Some Temple sacrifices involved worshippers gathering family and friends to consume a portion of the animal offered on the altar. By doing so the laity were made "partners in the altar" (1 Cor. 10:18), simultaneously deepening their experience of communion with God and each other. It was painful for Jewish Christians to be labeled as heretics and excluded from such communion.

Our author, however, reminded them that they did share in a sacrifice—Christ's sacrifice. Those who excluded them from the Tem-

---

4. Irenaeus, *Against the Heresies*, 4, 18, 5, as quoted in CCC 1327.
5. New International Version.

ple's sacrificial banquets had, ironically, by their rejection of Christ excluded themselves from partaking of food from the supreme altar. In the body of the epistle our author makes the argument that it was Christ's sacrifice—not those of the Temple—that had reached back through time to grant Israelites the forgiveness of their sins. Here, in the final chapter of his epistle, our author crowns his argument with the implication that believers in Christ eat from a far greater altar—the Cross—when they consume Jesus in the Eucharist. He continues this line of thought when he characterized Christian worship as a "sacrifice of praise"—something quite familiar to his first-century Jewish readership, but a subject of little consideration by modern Christians.

The Todah *of the Risen One*

"Sacrifice of praise" refers to the *todah*, a specific form of peace offering (Lev. 7:12–15).[6] The *todah* (Hebrew for "thanksgiving") was offered by one saved from the threat of death, which often came in the form of illness or persecution. In the *todah*, the one who had been saved praised God and celebrated the act of deliverance as a new beginning, the foundation for a new life, joyfully offered to God.[7] He brought an animal—a symbol of the life God had bestowed upon him—as well as unleavened bread. Portions of the animal and bread were offered by the priests at the Temple's altar. The one who had been saved then invited family and friends to the festal meal, where they would consume a portion of the sacrifice.

---

6. This is a common insight; I encourage the reader to consult the sections pertaining to Hebrews 13:15 in the following commentaries, available online: John Gill, *Exposition of the Old & New Testaments*; Matthew Henry, *Concise Commentary on the Whole Bible*; Robert Jamieson, A.R. Fausset, and David Brown, *Commentary on the Whole Bible*; H.D.M. Spence and Joseph S. Exell, eds., *The Pulpit Commentary*.

The Septuagint explicitly used "sacrifice of praise" to identify the *todah* (thank offering): "[Hezekiah said], 'bring near and offer sacrifices of praise in the house of the Lord.' And this congregation brought sacrifices and thank offerings into the house of the Lord" (2 Chron. 20:31); Lancelot C.L. Brenton, *The Septuagint with Apocrypha: Greek and English* (London: Samuel Bagster & Sons Ltd., 1851).

7. Hartmut Gese, *Essays on Biblical Theology*, trans. Keith Crim (Minneapolis: Augsburg Publishing House, 1981), 128–9.

The verbal element of praise was integral to the meal. It began with the blessing over the bread. Then, at the high point of the meal, the host lifted up a cup of wine—the "cup of salvation" (Ps. 116:13)—and verbally confessed (proclaimed) how God had saved him from death.[8] It was "a sacrifice of praise—the fruit of lips that openly profess his name" (Heb. 13:15).

The celebration of the *todah* underlies a number of the biblical psalms and, according to the *Mishnah*, played a prominent role in first-century Judaism.[9] From the time of David on, its importance steadily grew. When David brought the ark of the covenant into Jerusalem, he appointed a group of priests for the express purpose of offering *todah* and composed a psalm to mark the occasion (1 Chron. 16:4, 7–36, 41; Ps. 105:1–15).[10] The ancient rabbis invested the *todah* with such importance that they claimed it would continue long after all other forms of sacrifice became obsolete: "In the coming (messianic) age all sacrifices will cease, but the thank offering will never cease; all (religious) songs will cease, but the songs of thanks will never cease."[11]

Psalms composed for *todah* celebrations (such as Psalms 22, 40, 69, and 116) often follow a pattern. They begin in lament, with the faithful giving voice to their suffering and calling out to God for deliverance (e.g., "My God, my God, why hast thou forsaken me?" [Ps. 22:1]). They then turn to praise as the speaker looks confidently ahead to God's deliverance and the celebration of the *todah* (e.g., "From thee comes my praise in the great congregation; / my vows I will pay before those who fear him. / The afflicted shall eat and be satisfied; / those who seek him shall praise the Lord!" [Ps. 22:25–26]).

The early Church recognized how perfectly the *todah* psalms took flesh in Christ. In earlier chapters we saw the author of Hebrews quote from Psalms 22 and 40 (Heb. 2:12; 10:5–7). They were the psalms on Jesus's lips during his Passion: He sang Psalm 116

---

8. Ibid., 130.

9. Ibid., 131.

10. Michael Barber, *Singing in the Reign: The Psalms and the Liturgy of God's Kingdom* (Steubenville, OH: Emmaus Road, 2001), 76.

11. *Pesiqta Rav Kahana*, quoted in Gese, *Essays on Biblical Theology*, 133.

before departing for the Garden of Gethsemane[12] and invoked Psalms 22 and 69 while hanging upon the Cross.[13] The *todah* psalms were fulfilled superabundantly in Christ, whom the Father saved not just from the *threat* of death, but from *Sheol* itself (Ps. 16:10–11). And the Eucharist (*eucharistein*, Greek for "thanksgiving") that Jesus instituted at Passover, the night before he died, is the *todah* ("thanksgiving") feast he celebrates with the Church. The Lord celebrated it with the disciples at Emmaus, just hours after his Resurrection (Lk. 24:27–35).[14]

The Eucharist is where the Church joins Christ in giving thanks and praise to the Father for having saved him—*and through him, us*—from the curse of death. On the Cross, Jesus offered the life, divine and human, that he had received from the Father. Now, risen and ascended—himself still the offering—Jesus unites the Church to his offering under the signs of bread and wine. This is the most obvious way that Jesus functions as a priest in the order of Melchizedek—the way that the author of Hebrews apparently considered too basic to mention. (Recall that in Genesis 14:18–20 Melchizedek offered a *todah* of bread and wine on Abraham's behalf, after the latter's defeat of a vastly superior force.)[15]

12. "What shall I render to the LORD for all his bounty to me? I will lift up the chalice of salvation and call on the name of the LORD, I will pay my vows to the LORD in the presence of all his people. Precious in the sight of the LORD is the death of his saints. O LORD, I am your servant; I am your servant, the son of your handmaid. You have loosed my bonds. I will offer to thee the sacrifice of thanksgiving and call on the name of the LORD" (Ps. 116:12–17).

13. See discussion in Kapler, *Through, With, and In Him*, 76–80.

14. Note how Luke uses the same four verbs to describe both Jesus's actions at the institution of the Eucharist and the meal at Emmaus: took, blessed, broke, gave (Lk. 22:19, 24:30).

15. We see this point made in the early- and mid-third century writings of St. Clement of Alexandria (*Stromateis* 4:25) and St. Cyprian of Carthage (*Letter to a Certain Cecil*). We should not be overly surprised that the author of Hebrews would omit such an obvious connection; we find similar omissions elsewhere in the NT: The authors of the synoptic gospels recount how, on the Cross, Jesus prayed the first verse of Psalm 22; but they saw no need to point out how the piercing of Jesus's hands and feet and the soldiers' casting lots for his garments were prophesied in Psalm 22:16–18. Once the connection had been made between Jesus's death and Psalm 22, the three authors felt no need to state what should have been obvious.

We have noted time and again that the New Covenant's perfection consisted in providing, *in reality*, what the Old Covenant provided *only virtually*. The communion sacrifices of the Old Covenant represented Christ, but the communion sacrifice of the New *is Christ*. Under the New Covenant the bread and wine are converted into the sacrificial victim, so that Christians can join themselves, bodily and spiritually, to Christ's offering to the Father. The writer of Hebrews wanted his readers to understand that if they were to go back to the Temple sacrifices, they would trade the reality for its shadow (Heb. 10:1).

The Eucharist is the *todah*, or sacrifice of praise, par excellence, in which Christ *and the Church* continually confess God's saving action (1 Cor. 11:26; Heb. 13:15). The author of Hebrews illustrates this at the beginning of the epistle when he places the words of Psalm 22:22 on Christ's lips: "I will tell of your name to my brethren; *in the midst of the congregation I will praise you*" (Heb. 2:12). It was at the Last Supper, in the very act of instituting the Eucharist, that Jesus ensured that his sacrifice of praise would constitute the worship of the messianic age. There, in the midst of the Passover meal, he broke the bread, saying, "'This is my body which is for you. Do this in remembrance of me.'... 'This chalice is the new covenant in my blood. Do this, as often as you drink it, in remembrance of me'" (1 Cor. 11:24–25). Saint Paul assures us that "as often as you eat this bread and drink the chalice, you *proclaim* the Lord's death"—the act that saves us—"until he comes" (1 Cor. 11:26).

Christ, Our Passover Lamb

To understand the Eucharist further we must consider it in relation to the Passover. That sacrificial meal, where God's saving action at the time of the exodus was annually recalled, was a kind of national *todah*. By divine command, the Jewish people sacrificed unblemished lambs and then gathered as families to eat the lambs along with unleavened bread and bitter herbs (Exod. 12:26–27). The significance of each of the foods in relation to God's saving of the Israelites from slavery and the tenth plague was recounted; and God's saving deeds were sung in the *Hallel*, Psalms 113–118. (We already identified Psalm 116 as a *todah* psalm.)[16] One can surely recognize a similarity between the intent of the Passover meal and that of the *todah*. It is also worth noting that, of all the different types of sacrifices commanded in the Torah, the following stipulation was made only for the Passover lamb, the *todah*, and the sacrifice eaten at the ordination of priests: "let none of it remain until the morning, anything that remains until the morning you shall burn" (Exod. 12:10, 29:34; Lev. 7:15).

A unique element of the Passover, however, and one germane to our study, is its concept of "remembrance." In the Passover *Kiddush*, the blessing that followed the first cup of wine, God was praised for gathering his people in remembrance (*zikkaron* in Hebrew) of the exodus. *Zikkaron* was no mere memory exercise. It was a *ceremony* that made the past event present. The original night of Passover, when the angel of death passed over the homes of the Israelites and Israel's subsequent exodus, were one-time historical events; but the *zikkaron*, the Passover meal, recalled them and allowed every Jew born after that point to experience them too. How was that possible? The great "I Am" (Exod. 3:14) made it possible. When the Jewish people, like their ancestors, partook of the Passover lamb, unleavened bread, bitter herbs, and wine, they too were delivered from the threat of death in Egypt. By Jesus's time the Passover was also understood to look ahead to a future Passover night, when the Messiah would appear and definitively deliver Israel.[17]

The Eucharist perfects Passover. The unblemished passover lamb foreshadowed the sinless Christ (Exod. 12:5, 46; John 1:36, 19:33–34; Rev. 5:6–13). It was in the midst of the Old Covenant *zikkaron* that Christ established the New: "Do this . . . in *remembrance* (*anamnesis* in Greek, and *zikkaron* in Hebrew) of me."[18] Historically, Christ was "offered once" (Heb. 9:26); and yet, it was "through the *eternal*

16. The Passover, like the *todah*, was eaten in family groups, and recalled and praised how God saved the firstborn of Israel when the angel of death passed over Egypt, and the entire nation from slavery under the pharaoh. The Passover differed from the *todah* in that the former was a national sacrifice and ritual meal, while the latter was the sacrifice of an individual.

17. Thomas Nash, *Worthy is the Lamb* (San Francisco: Ignatius Press, 2004), 72.

18. 1 Cor. 11:23–25.

Spirit [that he] offered himself" to God (Heb. 9:14). His sacrifice, that of a divine Person, transcends history; it brings redemption to people of all times and places. Jesus appears before the Father with the wounds of his Passion still visible (Rev. 5:6). By doing so, he makes perpetual intercession for us (Heb. 7:25). When the Eucharist is celebrated here on earth, his Passover is re-presented to us, so we can join ourselves to his eternal offering.

Covenants had always been initiated (and renewed) through sacrifice. God and his people were united in the life of the sacrificial victim (Lev. 17:11). The act of sacrifice offered the victim to God, but the people had to take that life into themselves through a covenant meal. We see this at the first Passover (Exod. 12:1–14), where it was not simply the blood of the lamb that saved the firstborn of Israel, but *communion in its sacrificial flesh.* We see it again when Moses ratified the covenant at Sinai:

> [Moses] sent young men of the sons of Israel, who offered burnt offerings and *sacrificed peace offerings* of oxen to the LORD. And Moses took half of the blood and put it in basins, and half of the blood he threw against the altar. The he took the book of the covenant, and read it in the hearing of the people; and they said, "All that the LORD has spoken we will do, and we will be obedient." And Moses took the blood and threw it upon the people, and said, *"Behold the blood of the covenant which the LORD has made with you in accordance with all these words."* Then Moses and Aaron, Na'dab, and Abi'hu, and seventy of the elders went up, and they saw the God of Israel ... they beheld God, and *ate and drank.* (Exod. 24:5–11)

The New Covenant was sealed in Christ's blood. At his final Passover, Jesus echoed Moses—"This chalice which is poured out for you is the *new covenant in my blood*" (Lk. 22:20)—and he invited the apostles to eat and drink. Sacramentally, they ate and drank the same body and blood that Jesus offered the Father in his crucifixion and ascension.

Apart from the Eucharist, the contrast between Jesus's execution and the Jewish understanding of priesthood and sacrifice would have been almost insurmountable: Jesus was a Judahite, not a Levite. He offered his own life, not that of an animal, and died on a Roman cross outside Jerusalem instead of on the Temple's altar. *The institu-tion of the Eucharist* was where *Jesus interpreted his death* as the sacri-fice of the New Covenant; and it was the Jewish-Christian's ability to commune in that sacrifice that went farthest toward making Jesus's priesthood, and the sacrificial nature of his death, intelligible. The Eucharist cemented these basic truths and provided a ground for further theological reflection (like that found in the Epistle to the Hebrews).[19]

The Apostolic Witness

The Catholic Church claims nothing more for the Eucharist than the apostles did. Besides the record of its institution in the synoptic gospels of Matthew, Mark, and Luke, we also have the more devel-oped teachings of John and Paul.

The Apostle John's Eucharistic exposition is found in the Bread of Life Discourse. In terms of context, John linked Jesus's teaching to the Feast of Passover (John 6:4). In an attempt to prepare readers for the jarring statements in Jesus's discourse, John recounts two miracles. In the first, the multiplication of the loaves, John estab-lishes Christ's ability to defy the laws of nature as they pertained to bread; and in the second, Jesus's walking on water, John demon-strated Christ ability to defy the laws of nature with his body. Only after establishing those two points did John recount Jesus's startling claim: "I am the living bread which came down from heaven; if any one eats of this bread, he will live forever; and the bread which I shall give for the life of the world is my flesh" (John 6:51).[20] John reports how when listeners began objecting to Jesus's "cannibalistic" language, Christ became more explicit:

> Whoever eats[21] my flesh and drinks my blood has eternal life, and
> I will raise him up at the last day. For my flesh is real food and my

19. Albert Vanhoye, *Structure and Message of the Epistle to the Hebrews*, 13, 16; Scott Hahn, *Consuming the Word*, 24–5; Joseph Ratzinger, *Pilgrim Fellowship of Faith: The Church as Communion* (San Francisco, Ignatius Press, 2005), 94–7.

20. Jesus equated the flesh he gave in crucifixion with the flesh he would give in the Eucharist; they are either both figurative or both literal; David B. Currie, *Born Fundamentalist, Born Again Catholic* (San Francisco: Ignatius Press, 1996), 37.

21. The Greek verb is *trogein*, meaning "gnaws, chews."

blood is real drink. Whoever eats my flesh and drinks my blood remains in me, and I in them. Just as the living Father sent me and I live because of the Father, so the one who feeds on me will live because of me. This is the bread that came down from heaven. Your ancestors ate manna and died, but whoever feeds on this bread will live forever. (John 6:54–58)[22]

Jesus insisted on the literal interpretation of his words—at the cost of disciples (6:66). He even made this the subject of an ultimatum to the apostles (6:67).

The Apostle Paul witnessed to the same truths as John. In his First Epistle to the Corinthians he proclaims, "Christ, our Paschal Lamb, has been sacrificed. Let us, therefore, celebrate the festival" (1 Cor. 5:7–8). Later, after recounting Christ's institution of the Eucharist, Paul writes words that are inexplicable apart from the conviction that Jesus's body and blood are truly present in the sacrament:

Whoever, therefore eats the bread or drinks the cup of the Lord in an unworthy manner will be guilty of profaning the body and blood of the Lord. Let a man examine himself, and so eat of the bread and drink of the cup. For any one who eats and drinks without discerning the body eats and drinks judgment upon himself. That is why many of you are weak and ill, and some have died. (1 Cor. 11:27–30)

A person is not charged with murder for destroying a photograph, a mere image; neither would such grave chastisements be appropriate unless Christ was substantially present. Paul called the Corinthians' sharing in the Eucharistic bread and cup a *"participation"* in the body and blood of Christ (10:16). They received from "the table of the Lord" (10:21), an OT designation for the altar of sacrifice (Mal. 1:12). Like those in the Temple, they were made "partners in the altar" (10:18). And just as partaking of the Passover and *todah* sacrifices united worshippers to both God and one another, so the Eucharist creates the unity of the Church: "Because there is one bread, we who are many are one body, for we all partake of the one bread" (10:17).

---

22. New International Version.

But how can bread and wine be converted into the body and blood of Christ? The Catholic Church has used the term "transubstantiation," or "change of substance," to describe what happens when her presbyters pray Christ's words of institution.[23] The "substance," or that which gives the bread and wine their definitive identity, is completely converted into the substance of Christ's body and blood (which are inseparably united to his soul and divinity). The outward qualities, or "accidents," of the bread and wine remain— kept in place only by a continual act of will on the part of God.[24] This is not scandalous to the Catholic who understands that the universe, called into existence from nothing, is maintained in being only by an analogous act of God's will.

The Church does not presume to say *how* this change, indiscernible to our senses and instrumentation, occurs. She can only acknowledge that, as Jesus is our Creator, his comprehension of matter far exceeds ours. He can do with it whatever he wills. He made that abundantly clear when he multiplied the loaves, walked on water, appeared out of and disappeared into thin air after his Resurrection, and bodily ascended into heaven. The body and blood we receive in the Eucharist were formed in a virginal womb! To the majority of Jewish people in the first century, the suggestion that God would humble himself by becoming a man was the height of scandal; but the truth was that God's love caused him to descend even further— becoming the food of our bodies and souls. The Son chose to be born in Bethlehem (Hebrew for "House of Bread") and laid in a manger, a feeding trough for animals. "God chose what is foolish in the world to shame the wise" (1 Cor. 1:27); the Eucharist epitomizes the foolishness of the Cross. It exemplifies the faith for which the patriarchs were praised; Eucharistic faith is *truly* "the conviction of things not seen" (Heb. 11:1).[25]

The Catholic understanding of the Eucharist was the early Church's understanding of the Eucharist. Ignatius, Bishop of Anti-

---

23. See CCC 1375–6.

24. Matthew Levering, *Sacrifice and Community: Jewish Offering and Christian Eucharist* (Malden, MA: Blackwell Publishing, 2005), 157–8.

25. Ibid., 139.

och and disciple of the Apostle John, wrote of the Eucharist prior to his martyrdom in AD 110. He told his readers that he desired "the bread of God that is the flesh of Jesus Christ, of David's seed, and I want his blood as my drink."[26] He admonished believers in Philadelphia, Asia Minor, to "be diligent to use one Eucharist for there is [only] one flesh of our Lord Jesus Christ and one cup for unity in his blood. There is one altar as there is one bishop together with his presbyters, and deacons."[27] Ignatius cautioned the Church in Smyrna against those who "abstain from the Eucharist and from [set times of] prayer because they do not confess that the Eucharist is the flesh of our Savior Jesus Christ, that flesh which suffered for our sins but which the Father raised in his kindness."[28] Justin Martyr, the second-century apologist, recorded the early Church's Eucharistic liturgy (ca. 155). Anyone familiar with the Mass, as it is celebrated today, will recognize it in Justin's description:

> On the day we call the day of the sun, all who dwell in the city or country gather in the same place. The memoirs of the apostles and the writings of the prophets are read, as much as time permits. When the reader has finished, he who presides over those gathered admonishes and challenges them to imitate these beautiful things. Then we all rise together and offer prayers for ourselves ... and for all others, wherever they may be, so that we may be found righteous by our life and actions, and faithful to the commandments, so as to obtain eternal salvation. When the prayers are concluded we exchange the kiss [of peace].

> Then someone brings bread and a cup of water and wine mixed together to him who presides over the brethren. He takes them and offers praise and glory to the Father of the universe, through the name of the Son and of the Holy Spirit and for a considerable time he gives thanks (*eucharistian*) that we have been judged worthy of these gifts. When he has concluded the prayers and thanksgiving, all present give voice to an acclamation by saying: "Amen." When

26. Kenneth J. Howell, *Ignatius of Antioch and Polycarp of Smyrna: A New Translation and Theological Commentary* (Zanesville, OH: CHResources, 2009), 117–18.

27. Ibid., 124.

28. Ibid., 133.

he who presides has given thanks and the people have responded, those whom we call deacons give to those present the "eucharisted" bread, wine and water and take them to those who are absent.[29]

Justin goes on to explain, "For not as common bread nor as common drink do we receive these.... [T]he food which has been made into the Eucharist by the Eucharistic prayer set down by [Jesus], and by the change by which our blood and flesh is nourished, is both the flesh and the blood of that incarnated Jesus."[30]

The Ministerial Priesthood

Ignatius of Antioch and Justin Martyr make mention of those who presided at the Eucharist. Just as Israel was a priestly people, who nonetheless had a specific tribe who officiated at the Temple altar, so too the Church. There was a reason that the Levitical priesthood was part of God's covenant with Israel; it foreshadowed the ministerial priesthood to be established by Christ. With our understanding of the Eucharist's relationship to his priestly sacrifice on Calvary, we recognize how, when Jesus commanded the apostles to "Do this in remembrance of me," he was, in fact, ordaining them. He ordained them to a unique share in his priestly ministry on behalf of his Church.

For the Church to celebrate Jesus's sacrificial banquet after he returned to the Father, it was necessary that some members of his Body perform a special role. They, members of the Body, would serve the Body by acting in the place of Christ, the host of the Eucharistic banquet. The Eucharist is the offering of the "total Christ" (Eph. 4:13), Head and Body. Analogous to the human body, Christ the Head communicates orders and moves his "limbs" through a specialized, imbedded network of cells—a nervous system—ordained for this purpose. In the pages of the NT we find

29. Justin Martyr, *First Apology to the Emperor Antoninus Pius*, 65–67: PG 6, 428–29; quoted in *CCC* 1345.

30. Justin Martyr, *First Apology to the Emperor Antoninus Pius*, quoted in William A. Jurgens, *The Faith of the Early Fathers*, vol. 1 (Collegeville, Minnesota: The Liturgical Press, 1970), 55.

those who serve in this capacity referred to as apostles, bishops, presbyters, and those who assisted them, the deacons.[31]

John's account of the Last Supper complements the institution narratives of the synoptic gospels. In John, the language of Jesus's high-priestly prayer depicts his relationship to the apostles in terms of the high priest's relationship to the Levites.[32] As God gave the Levites to Aaron (the high priest) and his sons, to assist them in the priesthood (Numbers 3:9, 8:39, 18:6), so the Father gave Jesus the Apostles (John 17:6, 9, 24). John's Gospel employs the same verbiage as that found in the Septuagint's translation of the Book of Numbers.[33] The apostles' unique participation in Christ's priesthood is most clearly manifested when Jesus petitions the Father that they may share his priestly consecration: "for their sake I *consecrate* myself, that *they also may be consecrated* in truth" (John 17:19).

With these points in mind, John's account of Jesus washing the apostles' feet takes on added significance. Moses had been ordered to wash Aaron and his sons at the entrance to the Tabernacle in preparation for their ordination to the priesthood (Exod. 29:4).[34] John portrayed Christ as the New Moses, washing his apostles before their ordination to *his priesthood* (after the manner of Melchizedek). Christ ordained them when he entrusted them with the sacred duty of celebrating his *todah*/Passover by re-presenting his sacrifice under the signs of bread and wine.

---

31. See 2 Tim. 1:16; 1 Tim. 3:1–7; Titus 1:5–9; Acts 20:28; 1 Pet. 5:1; Acts 15:23–25; Acts 6:6; 1 Tim. 3:8–13.

32. Nicholas P. Lunn, "Jesus, the Ark, and the Day of Atonement: Intertextual Echoes in John 19:38–20:18," *Journal of the Evangelical Theological Society*, 52/4 (2009): 738–9. Lunn demonstrates this not just by considering the Greek texts of Numbers and John (for the verses indicated above), but even in Jesus's designation of Judas as "the son of perdition" who "perished" (John 17:12). It is the same Greek verbiage used in Numbers 16:33 and 20:3 to describe the punishment of those Levites (in a rebellion instigated by Korah) who tried to usurp the priesthood from the family of Aaron (Numbers 16:9–10, 40). Lunn's article can be accessed online at: http://www.etsjets.org/files/JETS-PDFs/52/52-4/JETS%2052-4%20731-746%20Lunn.pdf.

33. Ibid.

34. André Feuillet, *The Priesthood of Christ and His Ministers*, trans. Matthew J. O'Connell (Garden City, NY: Doubleday & Company, Inc., 1975), 164–5.

A ministerial priesthood was a prophesied element of the messianic age. Malachi, the last of the OT's twelve minor prophets, had said that the Messiah would *renew*—not abolish—Israel's priesthood: "[H]e will sit as a refiner and purifier of silver, and he will purify the sons of Levi and refine them like gold and silver, till they present right offerings to the LORD" (Mal. 3:3). Isaiah had also spoken of a priesthood in the messianic age, but added what must have been a bewildering detail for his Jewish audience—*Gentiles* would serve as *priests* and *Levites* (Isa. 66:21).[35]

We actually find the early Church using Temple nomenclature to speak of her ministers (ordained, as prophesied, from among the Jews and Gentiles). Clement, the third bishop of Rome, wrote his *Epistle to the Corinthians* within thirty years of the Epistle to the Hebrews. He reminded the church in Corinth how:

> [W]e ought to do in an orderly fashion everything the Master commanded us to fulfill in the properly established times. He commanded that the offerings and liturgical services be fulfilled, not in empty or disorderly ways, but at predetermined seasons and hours.... To the *high priest* belong particular liturgical services; the *priests* have their own places, and the *Levites* have their own ministries too. The layman is given orders appropriate for the laity. (40:1–2, 5)[36]

It does not take a great deal of imagination to discern the parallel between the ministers in the OT Temple and those in the New. The high priest corresponded to Christ, whose authority and priesthood were most fully manifested in the apostles and bishops. The priests, who like the high priest were ordained to offer sacrifice, represented

35. Saint Paul saw his own apostleship in priestly terms, linking it to the offering of the Gentiles. Paul said that he was given grace "to be a minister of Christ Jesus to the Gentiles in the *priestly service* of the gospel of God, so that the offering of the Gentiles may be acceptable, sanctified by the Holy Spirit" (Rom. 13:15–16). The prophet Malachi, although not as explicit as Isaiah, prophesied such an offering: "My name will be great among the *nations*, from *where the sun rises to where it sets*. In every place incense and pure offerings will be brought to me, because my name will be great among the nations" (Mal. 1:11, New International Version).

36. Kenneth J. Howell, *Clement of Rome and the Didache: A New Translation and Theological Commentary* (Zanesville, OH: CHResources, 2012), 113–4.

the council of presbyters; and the Levites, who assisted in the Temple, found fulfillment in the diaconate.

The Liturgy of Eternity

God told Moses that the Passover was to be observed *perpetually* (Exod. 12:14). The ancient rabbis intuited the same of the *todah*. The *tamid*—a lamb, bread, and wine—was offered on Israel's altar at the beginning and end of every day. All pointed ahead to the Eucharist that would subsume and perfect them by giving worshippers not just a figure, but a true, bodily participation in the *eternal* offering Christ makes of himself to the Father in heaven.

Early in this book we read the *Catechism of the Catholic Church*'s teaching that the Trinity is "the source of all the other mysteries of faith," and "the light that enlightens them."[37] We saw how the Son receives all he is from the Father, and makes a return of that love in the Person of the Spirit. We also saw how the Son achieved our redemption by becoming man and living, in his flesh, the offering he makes to the Father in his divine nature. Then, in the last chapter, we saw the saints in heaven participating in Jesus's eternal offering—prostrating themselves before the Father's throne and making a return to him of the life and graces He had given (Rev. 4:9–10). The saints participate in what can only be called an eternal *liturgy* (see Rev. 4:6–5:14).

We on earth are inserted into that liturgy when we celebrate the Eucharist. As Paul said, the Eucharist is our "participation" in Jesus's self-offering (1 Cor. 10:16). United to Christ, we are simultaneously joined with all our brothers and sisters in the heavenly liturgy. We already begin to do here on earth what we will do for eternity—participate in the eternal thanksgiving the Son makes of himself to the Father, in the Spirit.[38]

---

37. CCC 234.

38. Pope St. John Paul II wrote beautifully of the Eucharist's relationship to eternal life in his encyclical *Ecclesia De Eucharistia*: "Those who feed on Christ in the Eucharist need not wait until the hereafter to receive eternal life: they already possess it on earth, as the first-fruits of a future fullness which will embrace man in his totality. For in the Eucharist we also receive the pledge of our bodily resurrection at

Even now, the whole of our life is meant to be compenetrated by the Eucharist. Look at how the author of Hebrews joins the "sacrifice of praise" to our daily sacrifices: "[L]et us continually offer up a sacrifice of praise to God, that is, the fruit of lips that acknowledge his name. Do not neglect to do good and to share what you have, for *such sacrifices are pleasing to God*" (Heb. 13:15–16). This hearkens back to our discussion of justification: Christ acts in us, through the Spirit, to the pleasure of the Father. Our daily lives are an extension of the Mass, of Christ's sacrifice! We receive Christ's body and blood, soul and divinity, so that we can live *as Christ* in the midst of a hostile world. Observe how the author of Hebrews used Christ's words (Matt. 25:34–36) to remind his readers of their responsibility: "Let brotherly love continue. Do not neglect to show hospitality to strangers, for thereby some have entertained angels unawares. Remember those who are in prison, as though in prison with them; and those who are ill-treated, since you also are in the body" (Heb. 13:1–3). We owe this to one another, "for we all partake of the one bread"—Christ (1 Cor. 10:17).

the end of the world: 'He who eats my flesh and drinks my blood has eternal life, and I will raise him up at the last day' (John 6:54). This pledge of the future resurrection comes from the fact that the flesh of the Son of Man, given as food, is his body in its glorious state after the resurrection. With the Eucharist we digest, as it were, the 'secret' of the resurrection" (n.18). Text accessed at http://www.vatican.va/holy_father/special_features/encyclicals/documents/hf_jp-ii_enc_20030417_ecclesia _eucharistia_en.html.

7

The Authority
of the Church's Leaders

HEBREWS, CHAPTER 13

Obey your leaders and submit to them; for they are keeping watch over your souls, as men who will have to give an account.

$\sim$ *Hebrews* 13:17

✝

In this chapter we will draw together several threads. We saw in the last chapter how, even though all of the baptized share Christ's priesthood, those ordained to ministry do so in a distinct way for the benefit of their brothers and sisters. In this chapter we will discover how these ministers participate in Christ's kingship and prophetic/teaching ministry. When Jesus set out to renew Israel through the establishment of the New Covenant, he gave it twelve new patriarchs, the Twelve Apostles. The Apostles begot children for the Father through baptism, nourished them with Christ in the Eucharist, and "clothed" them in the confirmational graces of the Spirit (Lk. 24:49; Acts 8:14–17). If Jesus's Church is to have the Trinitarian unity for which he prayed at the Last Supper (John 17:20–22), it must remain united under the leadership of those whom the apostles ordained to succeed them, the pope and bishops.

I understand that this is a subject of disagreement among Christians, but it is a point that cannot be set aside. In an age of relativism, when Christianity's foundational beliefs are under attack from both within and without, we must direct our ears to those whom Christ ordained to speak for him. Just as God commanded the Jewish people to honor their fathers and mothers, so we Catholics have an obligation to listen to, and honor the directives of, our fathers in Christ (1 Cor. 4:14–15; 2 Cor. 6:13).

A Matter of Revelation

In the face of rejection from the powers-that-be, the author of Hebrews called the Jewish-Christian community to support one another (Heb. 10:25). Humility and obedience are prerequisites to Christian unity; and so, the author reminded the community of Christ's expectations: "Obey your leaders and *submit to them*; for they are keeping watch over your souls, as men who will have to give an account. Let them do this joyfully, and not sadly, for that would be of no advantage to you" (Heb. 13:17).[1] The verb translated here as "submit" literally means "to give way, yield."[2] God has laid a charge upon the leaders of his Church. They are to keep watch (in Greek, "go sleepless") in their care for souls.[3] Church leaders have been given a special share in Christ's governance of the Church. Like parents, they must exercise this duty over those entrusted to them whether we cooperate with their efforts or not. When they stand before Christ, they will be judged by how faithful, how courageous, they were in teaching us Christ's will and calling us to repentance and holiness.

We have used several images to describe Christ's Church: his Body, his Bride, his family. Each captures an essential facet of the truth. Throughout Jesus's public ministry, he spoke of the Church as the Kingdom of God.[4]

Jesus came into the world as the prophesied successor to David.

---

1. Paul made an almost identical plea: "But we beg you, brethren, to respect those who labor among you and are over you in the Lord and admonish you, and to esteem them very highly in love because of their work" (1 Thess. 5:12–13).

2. O'Brien, *The Letter to the Hebrews*, 529.

3. Ibid.

4. There are Christians who deny the identification of Christ's "Kingdom" with his "Church." For them the Church is merely of earth—a group of like-minded disciples, moving through time, while the Kingdom is Christ's reign in heaven and, finally, on earth at the end of history. Such a view, however, does not do justice to the incarnational and sacramental nature of Christian faith: The Word became flesh and, as we have seen in this study, uses created matter to communicate supernatural grace. To deny the identification of the Church with the Kingdom also requires turning a blind eye to the way Jesus uses the two terms interchangeably in Matthew 16:18–19, as well as how he spoke of his Kingdom containing sinners (see Matt. 13:47–48; 13:24–30, 22:1–14; 25:1–12), something that makes no sense if the

The angel who announced his birth said that Jesus would sit upon "the throne of his father David, and he will reign over the house of Jacob for ever; and of his kingdom there will be no end" (Lk. 1:32–33). That Kingdom was the theme of Jesus's preaching and the subject of his parables.

In structuring his Kingdom, Jesus looked to Israel's beginnings. From the crowd of disciples he called forth twelve, whom he named apostles (Lk. 6:12–13).[5] It was a momentous action on Christ's part, signaling that the time of fulfillment had arrived. As Israel arose from the twelve sons of Jacob, so his Church was to arise from the Twelve Apostles (Eph. 2:20; Rev. 21:14).[6] They would serve as his royal council, judges in his Kingdom (Lk. 22:28–29). "He who receives you receives me, and he who receives me receives him who sent me" (Matt. 10:40). The Apostles would share Jesus's responsibility of shepherding God's flock (John 21:15–17)—even, like him, to the point of laying down their lives (John 10:11, 15:12–13, 21:17–19).

Their greatness was to be found in service (Matt. 20:25–27). Part of that service was declaring actions allowable or disallowable for members of the community: "Truly, I say to you, whatever you bind on earth shall be bound in heaven, and whatever you loose on earth

Kingdom referred only to his heavenly or end-time reign. The answer lies in seeing the Church on earth as transitional, the Kingdom awaiting its full flowering. It *is* the Kingdom *but in seed form*—as in the parable of the mustard seed (Matt. 13:31–32). In the Our Father we pray for the Kingdom to arrive in toto. For additional commentary see William F. Albright and Christopher S. Mann, *Matthew: A New Translation with Introduction and Commentary* (Garden City, NY: Doubleday, 1971), 196–7.

Some may still object: "Christ told Pontius Pilate, 'My kingship is not of this world' (John 18:36), showing that his Kingdom is not earthly but spiritual." I reply that such a conclusion is not consistent with John's overall Gospel. Just a chapter earlier Jesus prayed, "[Father,] I do not pray that you should take [my Apostles] out of the world, but that you should keep them from the evil one. *They are not of the world, even as I am not of the world*" (John 17:15–16). If Jesus and the Apostles could be *in* the world but not *of* the world, then the same can be said of his Kingdom. It is physically, visibly present on earth; even though its origin and life are divine.

5. *Apostolos* in Greek, meaning "one who is sent."

6. God had also commanded Moses to make use of the leaders of the twelve tribes in his own time, to assist in conducting a census of the people, prior to war, and for making and breaking camp (Num. 1:4–17; see also 7:12–84, 10:14–27, 17:2–11).

shall be loosed in heaven" (Matt. 18:18). The same terminology was used by the rabbis of Jesus's day, and referred to their authority to declare teachings licit or illicit and actions as being in accordance with, or in violation of, the *Torah*.[7] If a member of the community wronged another, and repeatedly refused to repent, the apostles had the authority to place him outside of the community (i.e., excommunicate) in the hope of eliciting conversion (Matt 18:15–18). We find Paul exercising that authority in 1 Corinthians 5:1–5 and 1 Timothy 1:19–20.

The Master of the Palace

Among the Twelve, Jesus called Simon to a unique position of authority. Jesus met Simon's declaration that he was the Son of God with a declaration of his own: "Blessed are you Simon Bar Jonah! For flesh and blood has not revealed this to you, but my Father who is in heaven. And I tell you, you are Peter [*Petros* in Greek] and on this rock [*petra* in Greek] I will build my Church, and the gates of Hades shall not prevail against it" (Matt. 16:17–18).[8] In changing Simon's name to Peter, Jesus called to mind the change of Abram and Sarai's names to Abraham and Sarah (Gen. 17:5, 15) and that of Jacob to Israel (Gen. 32:28) during Israel's formative period. Simon's new name, like those of his ancestors, revealed the foundational role

---

7. J. Michael Miller, *The Shepherd and the Rock* (Huntington, IN: Our Sunday Visitor Publishing, 1995), 19; Stanley Jaki, *The Keys of the Kingdom: A Tool's Witness to Truth* (Chicago: The Franciscan Herald Press, 1986), 43.

8. For a look at the scholarship on the changing of Simon-Peter's name, especially from a non-Catholic perspective, see Scott Butler, Norman Dalgren, and David Hess, eds., *Jesus, Peter & the Keys* (Santa Barbara, CA: Queenship Publishing Company, 1997), 29–37. For example:

Gerhard Kittel's *Theological Dictionary of the New Testament* (Grand Rapids, MI: Eerdmans, 1968) is cited: "*Petros* himself is the *petra*, not just his faith or his confession. . . . The idea of the Reformers that He is referring to the faith of Peter [and not the man] is quite inconceivable."

Craig Blomberg, Baptist scholar and Distinguished Professor of New Testament at Denver Seminary, in *The New American Commentary: Matthew*, vol. 22 (Nashville: Broadman, 1992), wrote, "Peter's name (*Petros*) and the word 'rock' (*petra*) makes sense only if Peter is the rock and if Jesus is about to explain the significance of this identification."

God called him to play in Israel's rebirth.[9] Christ, the rock and cornerstone (1 Cor. 10:4; 1 Pet. 2:4–5), gave Peter a unique participation in his role as the foundation stone of the Kingdom. Jesus was not finished, though; he continued: "I will give you the keys of the kingdom of heaven, and whatever you bind on earth shall be bound in heaven, and whatever you loose on earth shall be loosed in heaven" (Matt. 16:19).

We saw above how Jesus granted the power to bind and loose to the Twelve, but Peter alone was entrusted with the keys of the kingdom. With that bestowal Jesus reinstated the office of the *asher al habbayith*, the master of the palace, originally established by King Solomon.[10] Jesus used the language of Isaiah 22, where the prophet foretold the removal of Shebna and succession of Eliakim to the office under King Hezekiah:

> In that day I will call my servant Eliakim the son of Hilkiah, and I will clothe him with your robe, and will bind your belt on him, and will commit your authority to his hand; and he shall be a father to the house of Judah. And I will place on his shoulder *the key of the house of David; he shall open, and none shall shut; and he shall shut, and none shall open.* And I will fasten him like a peg in a sure place, and he will become a throne of honor to his father's house. And they will hang on him the whole weight of his father's house.... (Isa. 22:20–24)

The master of the palace headed the list of royal officials and negotiated with foreign powers on the king's behalf (2 Kings 18:18; Isa. 36:3). The importance of the office was demonstrated when Prince

---

R.T. France, renowned Anglican scholar, in *The Gospel According to Matthew* (Grand Rapids, MI: Eerdmans, 1985) wrote, "The feminine word for rock, *petra*, is necessarily changed to the masculine *petros* (stone) to give a man's name, but the word-play is unmistakable (and in Aramaic would be even more so, as the same form *kepha* would occur in both places) . . . it is to Peter, not to his confession, that the rock metaphor is applied. And it is of course a matter of historic fact that Peter was the acknowledged leader of the group of disciples, and of the developing church in its early years."

9. Miller, *The Shepherd and the Rock*, 16.

10. Albright and Mann, *Matthew*, 196.

Jotham assumed the post during the illness of his father, King Aza-riah, prior to Jotham's own succession to the throne (2 Kings 15:5).[11]

The Old Testament background provides the needed context for understanding Jesus's statement to Peter. In Christ's Kingdom, Peter was appointed to the office of prime minister. It would be meaning-less to speak of the authority of other ministers apart from their unity with Peter. Jesus did not establish Peter as a dictator in regard to his brother Apostles, but as an older brother, granted authority to ensure unity. Peter's office, his possession of the keys, allowed him to speak the final word when matters of belief or discipline were in dispute, and in this way maintain the unity of the Church. He exer-cised this role at the Council of Jerusalem, when the Church debated whether Gentile converts were required to observe the Torah (Acts 15:6–11). The Church obviously has an ongoing need for this office. (Inherent in Christ's words to Peter was the promise of infallibility, which we will consider later in the chapter.)

When Peter was martyred in Rome during the reign of Nero, that city's bishop succeeded to Peter's office.[12] From the first century on, the Bishop of Rome has held the "keys" entrusted to Peter, with Jorge Mario Bergoglio (Pope Francis) now serving as Peter's two hundred sixty-fifth successor. Over the centuries, "pope" (from the Greek *pappas*, "father") became the most popular way of referring to the office holder. (In it, we hear an echo of Isaiah's "he shall be a father to the house of Judah" [22:21].) The idea of succession was implicit in Jesus's designation of Peter as master of the palace; the office had functioned that way throughout Jewish history. Peter was cognizant of the need for successors to the apostolic ministry, as evidenced by his move to replace Judas among the Twelve. Note Peter's wording:

> "[I]t is written in the book of Psalms . . . 'His *office* let another take' [Ps.109:8]. So one of the men who have accompanied us dur-ing all the time that the Lord Jesus went in and out among us,

---

11. Roland de Vaux, *Ancient Israel: Its Life and Institutions* (New York: McGraw-Hill Book Company, Inc., 1961), 129–30.

12. Ignatius of Antioch (110), Dionysius, Bishop of Corinth (170), and Tertul-lian (200) all left written testimony to Peter's Roman ministry.

beginning from the baptism of John until the day when he was taken up from us—one of these men must become with us a witness to his resurrection." ... And [the apostles and disciples] prayed and said, "Lord, who know the hearts of all men, show which of one these two you have chosen to *take the place* in this ministry and apostleship from which Judas turned aside, to go to his own place." And they cast lots for them, and the lot fell on Matthias; and he was enrolled with the eleven apostles. (Acts 1:20–22, 24–26)

There is more that must be said about apostolic succession, but first we must return to Jesus's public ministry and his appointment of still others to minister on his behalf.

The Elders/Presbyters

In structuring his Kingdom, Jesus looked not just to the times of the patriarchs and the monarchy, but to the Exodus. In addition to the apostles, Jesus selected seventy others whom he sent ahead of him to prepare villages for his arrival (Lk. 10:1). They mirrored the seventy elders, or heads of families, who, as we saw in the last chapter, accompanied Moses up Mount Sinai to seal the covenant in a ritual meal (Exod. 24:11), and were later given the Spirit to assist Moses in serving the people (Num. 11:16–25).[13]

Once the Israelites entered the Promised Land, the "elders" (*zeqenim* in Hebrew, *presbyteros* in Greek) formed a municipal council of sorts. Although often mature in age, the term was also applied to men of wealth and influence within the communities. Under the monarchy the elders regulated the life of the clans in their towns and villages (Ruth 4:2–9; 1 Sam. 30:26–31; 1 Kings 21:8; 2 Kings 10:1, 5; 2 Kings 23:1). They heard cases and rendered judgments (Deut. 21:19, 22:15).[14] When the elders could not reach a deci-

---

13. The connection between the seventy elders in the time of Moses and the seventy disciples dispatched by Jesus was apparent to the early Church. A number of Lukan manuscripts read "seventy-two" instead of "seventy," paralleling God's bestowal of the Spirit upon the seventy elders Moses gathered as well as two additional elders of the Lord's choosing (Num. 11:26–30).

14. Roland de Vaux, *Ancient Israel*, 138; Raymond E. Brown, *The Death of the Messiah*, vol. 2 (New York: Doubleday, 1994), 1428–9.

sion, cases were referred to a higher court in Jerusalem (Deut. 17:8–13; 2 Chron. 19:4–10), where religious cases were presided over by the high priest, and civil cases by the master of the palace (2 Chron. 19:11).[15] In the gospels we read of synagogue elders (Lk. 7:3); because the synagogue was under the patronage of the community, the synagogue and village elders were likely one and the same.[16] At the time of the Maccabees, elders, along with the priests and scribes, made up the *Gerousia* (Senate) under the leadership of the high priest. That body eventually came to be known as the Sanhedrin, which at the time of Christ consisted of the high priest and seventy other members.

All of this would have been in the minds of first-century Jews when Jesus dispatched his seventy disciples. He granted them the authority to heal the sick and proclaim the arrival of the Kingdom (Lk. 10:9). As with the Apostles, he assured them, "He who hears you hears me, and he who rejects you rejects me, and he who rejects me rejects him who sent me" (Lk. 10:16).

Because of their close association with Jesus, it seems likely that some, if not all, of the seventy were among the one hundred twenty who awaited Pentecost with the Twelve (Acts 1:15). It would also seem reasonable to posit that some would have been among the body of "elders" at the Council of Jerusalem (Acts 15:6). The critical decision reached there was promulgated on the authority of the Apostles and elders, indicating their level of responsibility in regards to the Church:

> The brethren, *both the apostles and the elders,* to the brethren who are of the Gentiles.... Since we have heard that some persons [from Jerusalem] have troubled you with words, unsettling your minds, although we gave them no instructions, it has seemed good

15. De Vaux, *Ancient Israel,* 153.

16. R. Alastair Campbell, *The Elders* (London, T.&T. Clark, 2004), 49. During the Sabbath synagogue service the elders sat at the front of the synagogue in a semicircle around the synagogue ruler. One of their functions was to act as a religious court with power to hand down sentences of excommunication and corporal punishment. Jesus made reference to this in Luke 4:20; John A. Kern, *A Study of Christianity as Organized: Its Ideas and Forms* (Nashville: Publishing House of the Methodist Episcopal Church, 1910), 211.

to us *in assembly* to choose men and send them to you with our beloved Barnabas and Paul.... For it has seemed good *to the Holy Spirit and to us* to lay upon you no greater burden than these necessary things...." (Acts 15:23–25, 28)

As Christ's Kingdom grew, so did its need for Christian elders,[17] or presbyters, in each community, who themselves were under the authority of the Twelve. (This mirrored the function of the elders under the monarchy, who referred difficult matters to the high priest or master of the palace in Jerusalem.) Both Peter and Paul referred to them as shepherds of God's flock (Acts 20:28; 1 Peter 5:1, 5). Like the elders of old, presbyters appear to have functioned as a council (1 Tim. 4:14). Paul's co-worker, Titus, was left in Crete for the purpose of appointing elders in every town (Titus 1:5). They were ordained through the laying on of hands (Acts 14:23[18]; 1 Tim. 5:22). Because of the presbyters' administrative role they were said to "rule," or "direct the affairs," of the local church (1 Tim. 5:17). [19] They were granted a share in the work of the apostles—preaching, teaching, anointing the sick, and absolving the sins of those who made confessions (Matt. 28:19–20; Tim. 5:17; John 20:22–23; James 5:14–16). It goes without saying that they would have presided at the Eucharist.[20] These were the leaders to whom the author of Hebrews expected his readers to submit. Anyone familiar with the Catholic Church will recognize this as the role carried out by her "priests." What many may not realize, however, is that a priest's official office is that of presbyter.[21]

To summarize our investigation thus far: Jesus established his Kingdom upon the Twelve Apostles, with Peter serving as his prime minister. Jesus appointed seventy to a second tier of ministry, which the early Church saw as corresponding to the historical function of

17. *Presbyteros* in Greek.

18. In Greek, the word translated into English as "appointed" in this passage literally means "to stretch forth hands." Scott Hahn and Curtis Mitch, *The Ignatius Catholic Study Bible*, 231.

19. New International Version.

20. In chapter four we saw how the Church in heaven was shown to John under the image of twenty-four *elders*, joined to Christ in the eternal liturgy (Rev. 4:4, 10).

21. "Priest," or *prēost*, is the Old English derivative of *presbyteros*.

elders/presbyters. Further, the Book of Acts and NT epistles show presbyters participating in the Apostle's ministerial priesthood and governance of the Church—exercising their ministry, like the Apostles, on behalf of the larger "kingdom of priests" (Exod. 19:6; Rev. 1:6). We are now in a position to speak of the other ministers we read of in the NT.

Bishops and Deacons

We often see the term *episkopos* (translated "bishop" or "overseer")[22] in connection with the presbyters. Most scholars believe that "bishop" and "presbyter" were used interchangeably in the early Church, the former referring to the minister's function (oversight) and the latter to his office (elder/presbyter). The terms are used in this way in Acts 20:17 and 20:28; and St. Jerome understood them to have functioned as synonyms during the lifetimes of the Apostles.[23] In Paul's pastoral epistles, however, some scholars interpret him as having made a distinction between the two.[24] "Presbyters," they point out, are spoken of in the plural; while "bishop" remains singular—possibly identifying the bishop as the head of the council of presbyters:

> This is why I left you in Crete, that you might amend what was defective and appoint *elders* in every town as I directed you ... a *bishop*, as God's steward, must be blameless ... he must hold firm to the sure word as taught, so that he may be able to give instruction in sound doctrine and also to confute those who contradict it. (Titus 1:5, 7, 9; see also 1 Tim. 3:1–7, 5:17)

Timothy and Titus, to whom Paul's pastoral epistles were addressed, certainly had oversight over the clergy they ordained; and thus, although the term was not applied to them in the pages of the NT, it

---

22. "Episcopal," derived from the Greek *episkopos*, is a term frequently heard in connection with Catholic and Protestant bishops.

23. Jerome, *Letter* 59.

24. R. Alastair Campbell, *The Elders*, 183–4; Kenneth E. Kirk, *The Apostolic Ministry: Essays on the History and the Doctrine of Episcopacy* (London: Hodder & Stoughton, 1946), 166–170.

is common for us today to refer to them as bishops. What we can say for certain, as we shall see in the next section, is that within forty years of Paul's writing, the bishop was recognized as the head of the local church and its presbyters.

Assisting the bishop and/or presbyters were the deacons (Phil. 1:1), an office created by the Twelve (Acts 6:4–6). Although the deacons' primary concern was seeing to the material needs of the faithful, they also preached and baptized (Acts 8:4–8, 12, 35–38). The deacon Stephen was so outspoken that he became the Church's first martyr (Acts 6:8–7:60). Paul listed qualifications for these ministers in 2 Timothy 3:8–13. Clement of Rome encapsulated the NT data in his *Letter to the Corinthians* (ca. 96):

> The apostles received the gospel for us from our Lord Jesus Christ ... they went out proclaiming with the confidence of the Holy Spirit that the Kingdom of God would come. Preaching in lands and cities, by spiritual discernment, they began establishing their first fruits, who were bishops and deacons for future believers. And this was nothing new because for many ages it had been written about bishops and deacons because as Scripture says somewhere, "I will appoint bishops for them in justice and deacons in faith" [Isa. 60:17, Septuagint]. (*Letter to the Corinthians* 42:1–5)[25]

Successors to the Apostles

Saint Paul had charged Timothy to guard the truth he had learned from him and to "entrust [it] to faithful men who will be able to teach others" (2 Tim. 2:2), i.e. the bishops and presbyters.[26] After the Apostles began dying, a transition had to take place. So long as Christ's Kingdom exists on earth, it will stand in need of the authority that Jesus entrusted to Peter and the Apostles—the keys of the Kingdom and the power to "bind and loose." The difficult subject of Gentiles and obedience to the Torah that was debated and settled at

---

25. Kenneth J. Howell, *Clement of Rome and the Didache: A New Translation and Theological Commentary*, 115. Dr. Howell points out that Clement's quotation of Isaiah is a loose rendering of the Septuagint's text.

26. Timothy, himself, had received this truth from Paul; see 2 Tim. 1:13–14.

the Council of Jerusalem was just the first of many core doctrinal issues in need of clarification. The post-apostolic Church needed the power to "bind" the Church to truth and "loose" it from error and heresy just as much, *if not more*, than the apostolic Church. Christ knew that the Church of the first and second century would face the Gnostics' denial of his humanity; and that the Church of the fourth would have to battle the Arian heresy regarding his divinity. The leaders of the fourth century needed apostolic authority to counter the Sabellianists' corruption of Trinitarian belief; and the Church of the fifth century needed that same authority to correct the Christological errors of the Nestorians and Monophysites. Every century has had its grave errors, demonstrating the Church's ongoing need of apostolic succession to address them.

As the Apostles' earthly journeys drew to an end, one man in each Christian community, the bishop, was recognized as their successor and accepted the responsibility for guiding the local Church and overseeing her presbyters and deacons. Clement of Rome's *Letter to the Corinthians* (ca. 96) identified such "apostolic succession" as the express will of Christ and the Apostles:

> Our apostles knew from our Lord Jesus Christ that there would be contention over the title of the bishop's office. For this reason, having received perfect foreknowledge, they appointed those mentioned before and afterwards gave the provision that, if they should fall asleep, other approved men would succeed their ministry. Now as for those appointed by them [the apostles], or by other men of high reputation with the approval of the whole church . . . we do not consider it right to eject them from ministry. (*Letter to the Corinthians* 44:1–4)[27]

The complete silence in which this transition occurred speaks volumes. Those who had known the Apostles were still spread throughout the Church, and the Apostle John was likely still alive as well. If it had been an innovation, unsanctioned by the Apostles, then there would have been a mass revolt. That is not what the historical record shows. Instead of protest, the letters of Ignatius of

27. Ibid., 117.

Antioch show us a Church united under the apostolic authority of the bishops.

Ignatius, the Bishop of Antioch, was a hearer of the Apostle John. In AD 110, while being transported to Rome for martyrdom, he dispatched seven epistles. In his parting words to the churches of Asia he stressed the role of the bishop in maintaining the unity of the Church:

> Your obedience to your bishop, as though he were Jesus Christ, shows me plainly enough that yours is no worldly manner of life, but that of Jesus Christ Himself, who gave His life for us that faith in His death might save you from death. At the same time, however, essential as it is that you should never act independently of the bishop—as evidently you do not—you must also be no less submissive to your presbyters, and regard them as apostles of Jesus Christ our Hope. . . . The deacons too, who serve the mysteries of Jesus Christ, must be men universally approved in every way; since they are not mere dispensers of meat and drink, but servants of the church of God. . . . (*Letter to the Trallians* 2:1–3)[28]

The obedience we Christians give to our bishops and priests is a manifestation of Jesus's obedience to the Father. Out of love for, and obedience to, the Father, the Son became obedient to a poor carpenter and a young maiden! We "obey [our] leaders and submit to them" (Heb. 13:17), not because they are smarter or more gifted than us; but because God appointed them as our shepherds, our spiritual parents (1 Cor. 4:15; 2 Cor. 6:13). We submit to them not just when they make pronouncements on questions of doctrine and morality, but even in purely disciplinary matters. The Church is the household, the family, of God; and a house or kingdom divided cannot stand (Lk. 11:17). Ignatius of Antioch reminded the Church in Philadelphia that

> [A]t the time I was with you, I cried out, speaking with a loud voice—the very voice of God—"Be loyal to your bishop and presbyters and the deacons." Some who were there suspected me of saying this because I already knew of certain dissensions among

---

28. Maxwell Staniforth and Andrew Louth, trans., *Early Christian Writings: The Apostolic Fathers* (New York: Penguin Books, 1987), 80.

you; but He whose prisoner I am will bear me witness that no such information had ever reached me from human lips. (*Letter to the Philadelphians* 7:1)[29]

Each of us, by our small acts of obedience, contributes to the unity of the universal Church: "Where the bishop is to be seen, there let all his people be; just as wherever Jesus Christ is present, we have the catholic Church" (*Letter to the Smyrnaeans* 8:2).[30]

Ignatius also bore witness to the position of leadership exercised by the church of Rome. He was effusive in his praise of her. She was "beloved and enlightened after the love of Jesus Christ . . . filled with the grace of God without wavering . . . filtered clear of every foreign stain."[31] Rome held "the *presidency* in the place of the country of the Romans." Ignatius noted the excellence of their teaching and example, asking "only that what you have enjoined in your instructions may remain in force."[32]

Above we read Clement of Rome's statement regarding apostolic succession. As the Bishop of Rome, Clement succeeded to the authority of Peter, the prime minister. Over a decade before Ignatius wrote, Clement's *Letter to the Corinthians* witnesses to the responsibility Rome felt, like Peter, for the Church at large. When the church at Corinthian deposed certain presbyters and violated the order established by Christ, Clement intervened:

It is shameful, indeed, very shameful, and things unworthy of your conduct, to hear of the very solid and ancient church of the Corin-

29. Ibid., 95.

30. Ibid., 103. This is the first written record we have of Christ's Church being called the Catholic (Universal) Church. It is interesting that it came from a citizen of Antioch, the same city in which Christ's disciples were first called "Christian" (Acts 11:26). The term "Catholic Church" spread quickly. In AD 155 *The Martyrdom of Polycarp* was addressed to all the dioceses of the holy and Catholic Church. The earliest list of books to be included in the New Testament, *The Muratorian Fragment* (AD 155–200) also spoke of the one Catholic Church, spread throughout the world.

31. Ignatius, *Letter to the Romans* 1:1; 3:1, quoted in Jurgens, *Faith of the Early Fathers*, vol. 1, 84.

32. Ibid., 86.

thians because of one or two persons are fomenting rebellion against the presbyters. (47:6)[33]

So you, therefore, having laid the foundation of this rebellion, submit to the presbyters and allow yourselves to be instructed for repentance, as you bow down the knees of your hearts. (57:1)[34]

When Christ gave Peter the keys of the kingdom and the power to bind and loose, he empowered Peter to act as his chief minister. Christ vested Peter's rulings with the authority of heaven (Matt. 16:19). Clement acted with this inherited authority: "But if there are any who refuse to heed the declarations He has made through our lips, let them not doubt the gravity of the guilt and peril in which they involve themselves" (59:1).[35] It was strong language; and yet, no one disputed Clement's right to speak in this manner, or to intervene in the affairs of a community over seven hundred miles away from his own. Instead, the Corinthians repented! Eighty years later, Dionysius, Bishop of Corinth, wrote to Clement's successor, Soter, telling him how Clement's letter was still read when the Church gathered for the Sunday Eucharist. Clement's words carried such force that they were read alongside Scripture.

To remain rooted in the teachings of Christ, we must remain faithful to the teaching of his bishops and their earthly head, the Bishop of Rome (the pope). A Christian does not appoint himself to the ministerial priesthood and apostolic ministry; he must be ordained to it by those who preceded him. This principle was enunciated in the Epistle to the Hebrews:

For every high priest chosen from among men is *appointed* to act on behalf of men in relation to God, to offer gifts and sacrifices for sins. . . . So also *Christ did not exalt himself to be made a high priest*, but was appointed by him who said to him, "You are my Son, / today I have begotten you"; as he says also in another place, "You are a priest for ever, / according to the order of Melchizedek." (Heb. 5:1, 5–6)

33. Kenneth J. Howell, *Clement of Rome and the Didache*, 120.
34. Ibid., 127.
35. Maxwell Staniforth and Andrew Louth (translators), *Early Christian Writings*, 47.

When Irenaeus, the Bishop of Lyons (France), argued against the Gnostics and other splinter groups who claimed to possess secret teachings of the Apostles, he directed them to the *authoritative repository* of Christ's truth. In his *Against the Heresies,* he listed the Bishops of Rome from the time of Peter and Paul up to the work's composition (ca. 189):

> Since it is too long to enumerate in such a volume as this the succession of all the Churches, we shall confound all those who, in whatever manner, whether through self-satisfaction or vainglory, or through blindness and wicked opinion assemble other than where it is proper, by pointing out here the successions of the bishops of the greatest and most ancient church known to all, founded and organized at Rome by the two most glorious Apostles, Peter and Paul, that Church which has the tradition of the faith which comes down to us after having been announced to men by the Apostles. *For with this Church, because of its superior origin, all churches must agree, that is, all the faithful in the whole of the world; and it is in her that the faithful everywhere have maintained the Apostolic tradition.*
>
> The Blessed Apostles [Peter and Paul] having founded and built up the church [of Rome], they handed over the office of the episcopate to Linus. Paul makes mention of this Linus in the Epistle to Timothy. To him succeeded Anacletus; and after him, in the third place from the Apostles, Clement was chosen for the episcopate. He had seen the Blessed Apostles and was acquainted with them. . . .
>
> To this Clement, Evaristus succeeded; and Alexander succeeded Evaristus. Then, sixth after the Apostles, Sixtus was appointed; after him, Telesphorus, who also was gloriously martyred. Then Hyginus; after him, Pius; and after him, Anicetus. Soter succeeded Anicetus, and now, in the twelfth place after the Apostles, the lot of the episcopate has fallen to Eleutherus. *In this order, and by the teaching of the Apostles handed down in the Church, the preaching of the truth has come down to us* (Book III, 3:2–3).[36]

---

36. Jurgens, *Faith of the Early Fathers,* vol. 1, 90. See how Irenaeus reiterates the principle that the touchstone of orthodoxy was the succession found in the ancient Churches.

Irenaeus goes on to state that those who succeeded to the Apostles' ministry received the "charism of truth."[37] This is what the Church refers to as the gift of infallibility, and it is of course attached to the pope in a special way.

Infallibility: Its Necessity and Limits

When Jesus was questioned by Pontius Pilate, he stated that he had been born to "bear witness to the truth" (John 18:37). At the Last Supper he promised the Apostles, "I will ask the Father, and he will give you another Counselor, to be with you for ever, even the Spirit of truth . . . the Holy Spirit, whom the Father will send in my name, he will teach you all things, and bring to your remembrance all that I have said to you" (John 14:16–17, 26). Saint Paul took the Lord at his word, telling his protégé Timothy that the Church was "the pillar and bulwark of truth" (1 Tim. 3:15). Paul went so far as to say that the Church was "the fullness of *the one who fills all things* in every way" (Eph. 1:23).[38] For the Church to be all that Christ and the Apostles claimed, it requires the gift of infallibility—a supernatural protection from teaching error. The Catholic Church believes that the pope, and all of the bishops of the world when they speak in union with him, are granted that gift.

We find the seeds of this dogma in Christ's promise to Peter: "I will give you the keys of the kingdom of heaven, and whatever you bind on earth shall be bound in heaven, and whatever you loose on earth shall be loosed in heaven" (Matt. 16:19). In terms of Peter's declarations on disciplinary matters—days of fasting, liturgical matters, excommunication or reinstatement—Christ's words are perfectly intelligible. When we turn to Peter's declarations on matters of belief and morality, however, Jesus's words only make sense if they presuppose a special divine assistance being given to Peter in such instances. The King, the Word made flesh, would not allow his prime minister to distort the truths he came to earth to reveal. Jesus respects the free wills of his ministers; but when Peter accepted the

---

37. Ibid., 96.
38. *New American Bible*, revised edition.

office of prime minister, he gave Christ the right to forcefully intervene in his execution of that office. Christ will prevent Peter and his successors from corrupting his Gospel—that is the dogma of papal infallibility.[39]

It is a very modest claim, and even then there are important caveats. Catholics believe that Christ ensures the infallibility of papal statements only when the pope speaks (a) in his official capacity as the successor of Peter; (b) with the intention of instructing the *entire* Church (not just his local congregation); (c) in matters of Christian doctrine (faith and morals).[40] All orthodox Christians feel comfortable affirming this, and far more, for the preaching of Peter and the Apostles. Likewise, the doctrines of inspiration and inerrancy—that the authors of Scripture wrote exactly what the Holy Spirit desired, in the words he desired, without any admixture of error—goes far beyond anything claimed for the pope. If one can affirm that such gifts were given to the writers of Scripture—especially Paul, Mark, Luke, James, and Jude, who were not numbered among the Twelve—then the Catholic claim for the pope is, relatively speaking, quite easy to accept.

Many mistakenly believe that infallibility means the pope is held to be incapable of sin.[41] We need look no further than the NT to see the error in such an understanding: Saint Paul wrote of how he had to publicly rebuke Peter for acting hypocritically. Peter, who with the help of the Holy Spirit had so boldly announced the Gentiles' freedom from the demands of the Torah (Acts 10:9–48; 15:7–11),

---

39. If you will excuse the crude analogy, we could say that if Peter and his successors act as the "tongue" of Christ's mystical Body, Jesus exercises the right to "bite down" on that tongue before it can say something false.

40. Papal infallibility obviously does not apply to statements a pope makes when delivering a homily at Mass, giving interviews, or commenting upon any subject other than faith and morals (e.g., science or politics).

41. Freedom from sin is not infallibility, but *impeccability*. Caiaphas, the high priest who delivered Jesus to death, exercised the gift of prophecy, purely in virtue of his office (John 11:49–52). Christ, with perfect foreknowledge, chose Judas to be one of His Twelve Apostles; Judas' subsequent betrayal did nothing to diminish the office of Apostle. In the same way, the personal sins of Peter and his successors does nothing to diminish the office of prime minister or negate the gift of infallibility.

drew back from table fellowship with Gentile Christians (and the eating of foods deemed unclean by the Torah) when the church at Antioch was visited by members of the "circumcision party" (Gal. 2:11–15). Peter did not fail in his proclamation of the truth, but in his living of it (something that all Christians find themselves guilty of). Even though Paul was compelled to confront Peter's sin, he nevertheless esteemed Peter's position as Christ's chief minister. Paul tells how, after his conversion and three years of prayer and study, he went up to Jerusalem and spent two weeks conferring with Peter (Gal. 1:17–18). After Paul and Barnabas began their mission to the Gentiles, a special revelation moved them to return to Jerusalem and lay out the gospel they had been preaching before Peter and the other Apostles. Paul, who had been taught the gospel by a special revelation of Christ, said he did this "to be sure I was not running and had not been running my race in vain" (Gal. 2:2). Christ desired that Paul's teaching be affirmed by his master of the palace.

If the Church's subsequent leaders, the pope and the bishops united around him, have not been granted the charism of infallibility, then Christ has shown himself to be a poor teacher indeed. The success of all human communication, education being an example, requires at least four elements: (1) a speaker/teacher, (2) a message, (3) a listener/student, and (4) an opportunity for the listener/student to ask clarifying questions of the speaker/teacher. Christ is the teacher, his body of teaching the message, and each individual Christian the student; but if Christ does not guarantee the infallibility of his ordained spokesmen, then he left no means for us to ensure a correct understanding of his teachings. Imagine how we would judge a teacher who began the school year by presenting each child with a textbook and the announcement, "I am going to spend today giving you a lecture on our assigned topic. After today, we will not have any further discussion, nor will I answer any questions. If you come to class daily and spend that time diligently studying your text, you should do well on the final exam." No one should dare to accuse Jesus Christ of doing something so outlandish! And as we have seen, he did not.

Jesus spent three years forming the leaders of his Church, promising the assistance of his Holy Spirit to take them deeper into the meaning of his words.[42] Then he sent them forth to act in his name and establish his Kingdom: "Go therefore and make disciples of all nations, *baptizing* them in the name of the Father and of the Son and of the Holy Spirit, *teaching* them to observe *all* that I have commanded you; and lo, I am with you always, to the close of the age" (Matt. 28:19–20). This is the work that Christ continues through the bishops and the presbyters and deacons who assist them.

---

42. When the pope and bishops look into the deposit of faith—Scripture and Tradition—and formulate a response to some question facing the Church, we deepen our understanding of Christ's message. The Church's subsequent infallible statements represent not an addition to Christ's teaching, something new coming from the outside. Rather, these statements are recognized as organic developments, the unfolding of what was already present, but in seed form. I submit that all Christians implicitly accept such development; an example is the Christian opposition to slavery.

Neither Jesus, nor the Apostles after Him, made any move to overturn the practice of slavery. (In fact, the Apostle Paul even counseled slaves to be obedient to their masters [Eph. 6:5; Col. 3:22].) While Roman and Jewish slaves seemed to receive better treatment than American slaves, there was still the utterly offensive premise that one human being could own another. How can we Christians today feel justified in our condemnation of this practice when Jesus and the Apostles didn't oppose it? Are we tacking on purely human opinions to the doctrine and morality of Jesus?

I maintain that we are not; the current stance is simply the full-flowering of that which was always implicit in the Gospel. Jesus gave the command "Love your neighbor as yourself," qualifying that all human beings are neighbors to each other (Lk. 10:25-37). He told us that we each should love each other so completely that we would be willing to lay down our lives for each other. Paul's Epistle to Philemon asked pardon for the runaway slave, Onesimus. Philemon was challenged to look upon Onesimus not just as a servant but as a brother in the Lord. Elsewhere, Paul wrote how, in Christ, there is no distinction between Jew and Greek, man or woman, slave or free (Gal. 3:28); all human beings have equal dignity in the eyes of God.

It took 1,800 years, but Christians finally applied these principles to the issue of slavery. If it is true that all men have the same dignity, and if we must love our neighbors as we would want to be loved by them, then there is no justification for slavery. We cannot claim a person as a possession; their dignity before God forbids it, and we would never desire to be someone else's possession. These principles were always implicit within the Gospel—just not taken to their logical end until much later.

The Bible and the Church

Outside of the Catholic Church there are millions of devout Christians born into, or brought to Christ by, Christian communities that do not recognize the teaching ministry of the pope and bishops. These communities do so through no fault of their own. The Catholic Church is candid in saying that the divisions that came about at the time of the Reformation were the fault of men on both sides.[43]

In place of the pope and bishops, these communities assert that the Bible is the *sole guide* for faith and morals, a belief known as *sola scriptura*. Theologians in these communities also speak of the "perspicuity" of Scripture, meaning that Scripture is clear to the ordinary reader and does not require explanation from an outside authority. We saw some of the serious objections to such a belief in chapter three: (1) abysmal literacy rates prior to recent centuries; (2) the dependence the majority of Christians have upon an authority to translate Scripture from Hebrew, Aramaic, and Greek into their native languages; (3) the positive value Scripture assigns to Tradition and the teaching authority of the bishops and presbyters; and (4) Scripture's outright denial of its perspicuity (2 Pet. 3:15–16; Acts 8:30–31). We should add that history has not borne out the Reformers' claims: the continual fracturing of Protestant communities, based upon the contradictory interpretations of Scripture arrived at by sincere, praying individuals, is abundant proof that Christ never meant for Scripture to stand alone.[44]

The canon of Scripture, however, is the most damaging argument against *sola scriptura* and the perspicuity of Scripture. Before "the Bible" can function as the sole rule of faith, it must first exist as a *fixed collection* of inspired works; and that did not happen until the fourth century. The *Epistle of Barnabas, Apocalypse of Peter, Shepherd of Hermas*, and *Didache*—all were read as Scripture by some com-

---

43. See Vatican Council II's *Unitatis Redintegratio* (*Decree on Ecumenism*), no. 3, at http://www.vatican.va/archive/hist_councils/ii_vatican_council/documents/vat-ii_decree_19641121_unitatis-redintegratio_en.html.

44. That these communities see the ongoing need for pastors to deliver weekly lessons from Scripture, as well as "Sunday school," would also seem a strong argument against the perspicuity of Scripture.

munities in the early Church, while the inspiration of other books (1 Peter, 2 Peter, Jude, 2 John, 3 John, the Apocalypse of John) were disputed or denied.[45] It was Sacred Tradition—which books had been accepted and their inspiration witnessed to by inclusion in the Sunday Eucharist—and the popes and bishops of the Catholic Church who authoritatively proclaimed a New Testament canon of twenty-seven books (and an Old Testament canon of forty-six).

Saint Augustine of Hippo pointed this out, in the fourth century, to the Manichæans with whom he was debating:

> Perhaps you will read the gospel to me, and will attempt to find there a testimony to Manichæus. But *should you meet with a person not yet believing the [books of the] gospel, how would you reply to him* were he to say, "I do not believe"? *For my part, I should not believe the gospel except as moved by the authority of the Catholic Church.* So when those on whose authority I have consented to believe in the gospel tell me not to believe in Manichæus, how can I but consent? . . . If you say, Do not believe the Catholics: you cannot fairly use the gospel in bringing me to faith in Manichæus; for it was at the command of the Catholics that I believed the gospel.[46]

Scripture and the authoritative Tradition preserved and taught by the popes and bishops are interlocked. Apart from the binding authority of the pope and bishops, the most a Christian can claim for the Bible is that it is a *fallible collection* of infallible books.[47] Whenever a Christian says, "Jesus taught...," or "the Apostle Paul taught...," he or she is actually saying, "*The bishops of the Church assure me that* Jesus taught..., that Paul taught..." That is the historical reality. As the nineteenth-century convert John Henry Newman was forced to conclude—and hopefully, after our own brief investigation, you will concur—"To be deep in history is to cease to be Protestant."[48]

---

45. See Appendix.

46. Augustine, *Against the Epistle of Manichæus, Called Fundamental* 5:6, accessed at http://www.ccel.org/ccel/schaff/npnf104.iv.viii.vi.html.

47. R.C. Sproul, *Now That's A Good Question!* (Wheaton, Illinois: Tyndale Publishers, Inc., 1996), 82.

48. John Henry Newman, *An Essay on the Development of Christian Doctrine* (Notre Dame, IN: University of Notre Dame Press, 1989), 8.

The Fullness of Truth

Truth is trinitarian. The One God exists as a three-fold, reciprocal relationship of love; and the fullness of his truth is guaranteed to us *through the reciprocal relationship* existing between Scripture, Tradition, and the teaching office of the Church. We are meant to receive God's word from the Apostle's successors, in the midst of the Eucharistic celebration, united with the most holy Trinity and the whole communion of saints through Christ's sacrificial body and blood. However direct, however deep the personal relationship between Jesus and the individual Christian, the Lord has made us members of a *people*; and he has made us dependent upon other members of that people to receive the fullness of his truth.[49] The Church is his partner, his Bride; and we cannot truly know his mind, without knowing her, without submitting to the authoritative teaching and directives of Christ's ordained shepherds; so "[o]bey your leaders and submit to them; for they are keeping watch over your souls, as men who will have to give an account" (Heb. 13:17).

---

49. If one continues to doubt this, consider how the Lord made the evangelization of the Americas dependent upon the missionary efforts of the Church in the sixteenth century.

Conclusion

Remember those who are in prison, as though in prison with them; and those who are ill-treated, since you also are in the body. Let marriage be held in honor among all, and let the marriage bed be undefiled; for God will judge the immoral and adulterous. Keep your life free from love of money, and be content with what you have; for he has said, "I will never fail you nor forsake you" [Deut. 31:6; Jos. 1:5]. Hence we can confidently say, "The Lord is my helper, I will not be afraid; what can man do to me?" [Ps. 118:6]

                                                  —Hebrews 13:3–6

✝

In the six months spent writing these pages, I have been shocked by how quickly the struggles facing the Church today are coming to resemble those faced by the Church of the first century: Christians in the Middle East and Africa are being killed, for no other reason than their faith in Christ; here in the United States, the land of religious freedom, the moral convictions of Christian business owners are making them the targets of smear campaigns and economic fines. The word that God communicated through the author of Hebrews is a living word; it addresses disciples in the twenty-first century as much as disciples in the first, reminding us that we "share in Christ" only if we "hold our first confidence firm to the end" (Heb. 3:14; see also 6:4–6 and 10:28–29). We in the West must do all we can to speak Christ's truth to a disintegrating, increasingly illogical culture. We must address ourselves to those without faith, doing our best to reawaken them to the sanctity of human life and the demands of the natural law. As a tremendous help in this endeavor, let me direct you once again to Dr. Kevin Vost's companion volume, *The Porch and the Cross: Ancient Stoic Wisdom for Modern Christian Living.*

Hebrews makes no attempt to gloss over the difficulties inherent to living as a disciple of Christ: "you have need of endurance, so that you may do the will of God and receive what is promised" (10:36). Financial ruin and martyrdom are not the greatest threats facing us. Jesus was blunt: "[D]o not fear those who kill the body but cannot kill the soul; rather fear him who can destroy both soul and body in hell" (Matt. 10:28).

If history holds true, then the more that darkness tries to envelope the Church, the more brightly she will shine with the grace and truth of Christ. I write these words having just returned from the Easter Vigil, where I saw twenty-two people enter Christ's Catholic Church. I witnessed their "yes" to all the means of grace we encountered in our study of Hebrews—and the countless others that God has awaiting them.

To face the difficulties that seem to lie ahead, we need to imitate those twenty-two souls by laying claim to the fullness of God's truth and the fullness of the means of salvation; and the Epistle to the Hebrews has already given us a wonderful introduction. We need God's word in its entirety—all seventy-three books of Scripture, read in the light of Sacred Tradition. We need the authoritative teaching of the pope and bishops to counter the distortion of Christ's message that we hear from far too many pulpits—political and religious. We need the courageous example and the intercession of the great saints who trod this path before us. Most importantly we need the supernatural strength of the sacraments, especially the Eucharist, where we unite ourselves to Christ in his Passover from this world to the Father.

Both individually and corporately, the members of Christ's Body are destined to join him in his death and resurrection to glory. It is inevitable:

> Before Christ's second coming the Church must pass through a final trial that will shake the faith of many believers [Luke 18:8; Matt. 24:12]. . . . [It] will unveil the "mystery of iniquity" in the form of a religious deception offering men an apparent solution to their problems at the price of apostasy from the truth. The supreme religious deception is that of the Antichrist, a pseudo-messianism by which man glorifies himself in place of God and of his Messiah come in the flesh. . . . The Church will enter the glory

of the kingdom only through this final Passover, when she will follow her Lord in his death and Resurrection [2 Thess. 2:4–12; 1 Thess. 5:2–3; 2 John 7; 1 John 2:18, 22]. The kingdom will be fulfilled, then, not by a historic triumph of the Church through a progressive ascendancy, but only by God's victory over the final unleashing of evil, which will cause his Bride to come down from heaven. (CCC 675, 677)

In a divine paradox, that final persecution will not be the Church's defeat, but her victory. The Lion of Judah, Christ Jesus, never roared more loudly than in his silence as the sacrificial lamb (Rev. 5:5; Isa. 53:7); and the same will be true of the Church. Then the power of his Resurrection will burst forth as the Church on earth, with bodies glorified, meet the Church of heaven, and together celebrate the arrival of the heavenly Jerusalem (1 Cor. 15:51–58; Rev. 21:1–7).

Before that final day, though, when the Church faces her greatest trial, it will be her Jewish brothers and sisters who reinvigorate her. Saint Paul promised that, because "the gifts and the call of God are irrevocable" (Rom. 11:29), the Jewish people will recognize their Messiah. It is a point of Catholic Faith:

> The glorious Messiah's coming is suspended at every moment of history until his recognition by "all Israel" [Rom. 11:20–16; cf. Matt. 23:39]. . . . The "full inclusion" of the Jews in the Messiah's salvation, in the wake of "the full number of the Gentiles" [Rom. 11:12, 25; cf. Lk 21:24], will enable the People of God to achieve "the measure of the stature of the fullness of Christ," in which "God may be all in all" [Eph. 4:13; 1 Cor. 15:28]. (CCC 674)

The conflict that occasioned the writing of the Epistle to the Hebrews—the tension between those Jews who recognized Jesus as the Messiah and those who did not—will be fully overcome as the children of Abraham, Isaac, and Jacob visibly take their place in the Body of their brother, Jesus. Together, Jew and Gentile, we will celebrate Jesus's *todah* and participate in his Passover to the Father.

Whether that day is near or still far off, the prayer that the author of Hebrews offered for his readers is the same that I offer for you:

> Now may the God of peace who brought again from the dead our Lord Jesus, the great shepherd of the sheep, by the blood of the

eternal covenant, equip you with everything good that you may do his will, working in you that which is pleasing in his sight, through Jesus Christ; to whom be glory for ever and ever. Amen. (Heb. 13:20–21)

Appendix
Formation of the New Testament's Canon

Year AD	Author	Location	Work in which information is found	Canon or Comments
155–200	Unknown	Unknown, possibly Rome	*The Muratorian Fragment*	Canon + Wisdom + Apocalypse of Peter – Hebrews –James –1 Peter –3 John –2 Peter
190–210	St. Clement, director of the school of catechumens	Alexandria, Egypt	*Sketches*	Canon + Epistle of Barnabas + Apocalypse of Peter
226–232	Origen	Probably Alexandria	*Commentaries on John*	Comment: Calls 2 Peter's authenticity doubtful
300–325	Eusebius Pamphilus, Bishop of Caesarea	Palestine	*History of the Church*, Book III	Comment Labels as "disputed" James, Jude, 2 Peter, 2 John, 3 John. Labels as "spurious" Acts of Paul, The Shepherd, Apocalypse of Peter, Epistle of Barnabas, Didache, and *Apocalypse of John* (Revelation).
343–381	Council of Laodicea (Note: local council, NOT Ecumenical Council, thus NOT an infallible statement.)	Phrygia, Asia Minor	*Canons* [or Rulings] *of Laodicea*	Canon –Apocalypse of John (Book of Revelation)
350	St. Cyril, Bishop of Jerusalem	Palestine	*Catechetical Lectures*	Canon –Apocalypse of John (Book of Revelation)

Year AD	Author	Location	Work in which information is found	Canon or Comments
367	St. Athanasius, Bishop of Alexandria	Alexandria, Egypt	*Thirty-Ninth Festal Letter*	CURRENT CANON
380	St. Ampholichius of Iconium, Bishop	Iconium (Present-day Turkey)	*Iambic Letter to Seleucus*	Comment: "Of the Catholic epistles, some say seven need be accepted, others only three: one of James, one of Peter, one of John, —or three of John and with them two of Peter, —the seventh that of Jude. The Apocalypse of John some accept, but most will call it spurious. . . ."
382	St. Damasus I, Pope	Rome, Italy	*The Decrees of Damasus*[a]	CURRENT CANON
383–389	St. Gregory of Nazianz, Bishop	Arianz, Eastern Asia Minor	*Collected Poems*	Canon – Apocalypse of John
393	Council of Hippo	Hippo, Africa	*Canons of the Council of Hippo*	CURRENT CANON
397	St. Augustine, Bishop of Hippo	Hippo, Africa	*Christian Instruction*	CURRENT CANON
405	Innocent I, Pope	Rome, Italy	*Letter to Exsuperius* (Bishop of Toulouse)[b]	CURRENT CANON
419	Council of Carthage (local council, presided over by St. Augustine; because its minutes were approved by the Pope, however, most Christians appear to have felt bound by its decision on the canon).	Carthage, Africa	*Canons of the Council of Carthage*	CURRENT CANON

Appendix

a. *The Decree of Damasus* appears to have originally been part of the Decrees of the Council of Rome (a local council, not ecumenical). As such it is not considered an infallible statement. Remember, to be considered infallible, the Pope must (a) speak from his office as the successor of Peter, (b) teach on a matter of faith or morals, and (c) do so with the clear intention that what he says be considered binding upon *all* Christians. Because of the Pope's role within the Church, everything he teaches should be given consideration by a Christian; but only those things which are taught in the above manner are considered infallible.

b. Again, a letter from the pope to another bishop does not constitute an infallible statement of belief.

Bibliography

Akin, James. *The Salvation Controversy*. El Cajon, CA: Catholic Answers Press, 2001.

———. *The Drama of Salvation*. El Cajon, CA: Catholic Answers Press, 2015.

Albright, William F. and Christopher S. Mann. *Matthew: A New Translation with Introduction and Commentary*. Garden City, NY: Doubleday, 1971.

Augustine. *Against the Epistle of Manichæus, Called Fundamental*. http://www.ccel.org/ccel/schaff/npnf104.iv.viii.vi.html.

Barber, Michael. *Singing in the Reign: The Psalms and the Liturgy of God's Kingdom*. Steubenville, OH: Emmaus Road, 2001.

Brenton, Lancelot C. L. *The Septuagint with Apocrypha: Greek and English*. London: Samuel Bagster & Sons Ltd., 1851.

Brown, Raymond E. *The Death of the Messiah, Vol. 2*. New York: Doubleday, 1994.

Butler, Scott, Norman Dalgren, and David Hess, eds. *Jesus, Peter & the Keys*. Santa Barbara, CA: Queenship Publishing Company, 1997.

Catechism of the Catholic Church. 2nd ed. Vatican City: Libreria Editrice Vaticana, 1997.

Campbell, R. Alastair. *The Elders*. London, T. & T. Clark, 2004.

Currie, David B. *Born Fundamentalist, Born Again Catholic*. San Francisco: Ignatius Press, 1996.

De Vaux, Roland. *Ancient Israel: Its Life and Institutions*. New York: McGraw-Hill Book Company, Inc., 1961.

Encyclopaedia Judaica. Jerusalem: Keter Publishing House, 1972.

Feingold, Lawrence. *The Mystery of Israel and the Church, Vol. I: Figure and Fulfillment*. St. Louis: The Miriam Press, 2010.

———. *The Mystery of Israel and the Church, Vol. II: Things New and Old*. St. Louis: The Miriam Press, 2010.

———. *The Mystery of Israel and the Church, Vol. III: The Messianic Kingdom of Israel*. St. Louis: The Miriam Press, 2010.

Feuillet, André. *The Priesthood of Christ and His Ministers*. Translated by Matthew J. O'Connell. Garden City, NY: Doubleday & Company, Inc., 1975.

Flannery, Austin. *Vatican Council II: The Conciliar and Post Conciliar Documents*. Northport, NY: Costello Publishing Company, 1992.

Gese, Hartmut. *Essays on Biblical Theology*. Translated by Keith Crim. Minneapolis: Augsburg Publishing House, 1981.

Girdlestone, Robert R. *Synonyms of the Old Testament*. Grand Rapids, MI: Wm. B. Eerdmans Publishing Co., 1948.

Hahn, Scott. *Consuming the Word: The New Testament and the Eucharist in the Early Church*. New York: Image, 2013.

———. *Hail Holy Queen: The Mother of God in the Word of God*. San Francisco: Doubleday, 2001.

Hahn, Scott and Curtis Mitch. *The Ignatius Catholic Study Bible: New Testament*. San Francisco: Ignatius Press, 2010.

Howell, Kenneth J. *Ignatius of Antioch and Polycarp of Smyrna: A New Translation and Theological Commentary*. Zanesville, OH: CHResources, 2009.

———. *Clement of Rome and the Didache: A New Translation and Theological Commentary*. Zanesville, OH: CHResources, 2012.

Jaki, Stanley. *The Keys of the Kingdom: A Tool's Witness to Truth*. Chicago: The Franciscan Herald Press, 1986.

John of the Cross. *The Collected Works of St. John of the Cross*. Translated by Kieran Kavanaugh and Otilio Rodriguez. Washington, DC: Institute of Carmelite Studies, 1991.

John Paul II. *Ecclesia De Eucharistia*. http://www.vatican.va/holy_father/special_features/encyclicals/documents/hf_jp-ii_enc_20030417_ecclesia_eucharistia_en.html.

Johnson, Luke Timothy. *Hebrews: A Commentary (The New Testament Library)*. Louisville, KY: Westminster John Knox Press, 2006.

Johnston, Philip S. *Shades of Sheol: Death and Afterlife in the Old Testament*. Downers Grove, IL: InterVarsity Press, 2002.

Jurgens, William A. *The Faith of the Early Fathers, Vol. 1*. Collegeville, MN: The Liturgical Press, 1970.

Kapler, Shane. *The God Who is Love: Explaining Christianity From Its Center*. St. Louis: Out of the Box, 2009.

———. *Through, With, and In Him: The Prayer Life of Jesus and How to Make It Our Own*. Kettering, OH: Angelico Press, 2014.

Kereszty, Roch A. *Jesus Christ: Fundamentals of Christology*. New York: Alba House, 1991.

Kern, John A. *A Study of Christianity as Organized: Its Ideas and Forms*. Nashville: Publishing House of the Methodist Episcopal Church, 1910.

Kirk, Kenneth E. *The Apostolic Ministry: Essays on the History and the Doctrine of Episcopacy*. London: Hodder & Stoughton, 1946.

Kodell, Jerome. *The Eucharist in the New Testament*. Collegeville, MN: The Liturgical Press, 1988.

Koester, Craig R. *Hebrews: A New Translation with Introduction: The Anchor Bible*. New York: Doubleday, 2001.

Law, Timothy Michael. *When God Spoke Greek: The Septuagint and the Making of the Christian Bible*. New York: Oxford University Press, 2013.

Levering, Matthew. *Sacrifice and Community: Jewish Offering and Christian Eucharist*. Malden, MA: Blackwell Publishing, 2005.

Lunn, Nicholas P. "Jesus, the Ark, and the Day of Atonement: Intertextual Echoes in John 19:38–20:18." *Journal of the Evangelical Theological Society*, 52/4, 2009.

Mason, Eric F. and Kevin B. McCruden, eds. *The Epistle to the Hebrews: A Resource for Students*. Atlanta: Society of Biblical Literature, 2011.

McDonald, Lee Martin and James A. Sanders. *The Canon Debate*. Peabody, MA: Hendrickson Publishers, Inc., 2002.

Meier, John P. *A Marginal Jew: Rethinking the Historical Jesus, Vol. 1*. New York: Doubleday, 1991.

Miller, J. Michael. *The Shepherd and the Rock*. Huntington, IN: Our Sunday Visitor Publishing, 1995.

Miravalle, Mark, ed. *Mariology: A Guide for Priests, Deacons, Seminarians, and Consecrated Persons*. Goleta, CA: Queenship Publishing, 2007.

Moore, George Foot. *Judaism in the First Centuries of the Christian Era, Vol. 2*. New York: Schocken Books, 1971.

Most, William G. *Free From All Error*. Libertyville, IL: Prow Books/Franciscan Marytown Press, 1985.

Nash, Thomas. *Worthy is the Lamb*. San Francisco: Ignatius Press, 2004.

Newman, John Henry. *An Essay on the Development of Christian Doctrine*. Notre Dame, IN: University of Notre Dame Press, 1989.

O'Brien, Peter J. *The Letter to the Hebrews*. Grand Rapids, MI: Wm. B. Eerdmans Publishing Co., 2010.

O'Collins, Gerald. *Christology: A Biblical, Historical, and Systematic Study of Jesus*. New York: Oxford University Press, 1995.

O'Connor, James T. *The Father's Son*. Boston: St. Paul Books & Media, 1984.

Organ, Barbara. *Is the Bible Fact or Fiction?: An Introduction to Biblical Historiography*. New York: Paulist Press, 2004.

Ratzinger, Joseph. *Eschatology: Death and Eternal Life*. Washington, DC: The Catholic University of America Press, 2007.

———. *Pilgrim Fellowship of Faith: The Church as Communion*. San Francisco: Ignatius Press, 2005.

Staniforth, Maxwell and Andrew Louth, trans. *Early Christian Writings: The Apostolic Fathers.* New York: Penguin Books, 1987.

Staples, Tim. *Behold Your Mother: A Biblical and Historical Defense of the Marian Doctrines.* El Cajon, CA: Catholic Answers Press, 2014.

Sheed, Frank J. *Theology and Sanity.* San Francisco: Ignatius Press, 1993.

———. *Theology for Beginners.* Brooklyn, NY: Angelico Press, 2013.

Sproul, R.C. *Now That's A Good Question!* Wheaton, IL: Tyndale Publishers, Inc., 1996.

Strong, James. *A Concise Dictionary of the Words in the Hebrew Bible.* New York: Abingdon Press, 1890.

Vanhoye, Albert. *Structure and Message of the Epistle to the Hebrews.* Rome: Editrice Pontificia Universita Gregoriana, 1989.

Wise, Michael, Martin Abegg, Jr., and Edward Cook. *The Dead Sea Scrolls: A New Translation.* New York: Harper Collins Publishers, 1995.

Wright, N.T. *Hebrews for Everyone.* Louisville, KY: Westminster John Knox Press, 2004.

Made in the USA
Coppell, TX
14 March 2021